Poetry Aotearoa Yearbook

Poetry Aotearoa Yearbook

2023

Edited by Tracey Slaughter

MASSEY UNIVERSITY PRESS

Contents

ESSAYS

REVIEWS

Editorial

Poetry Aotearoa: Poem as encounter

> That space asks for something to enter it.
> — Tessa Keenan

When the crises of our past years closed so many doors, it's not hard to see why we reached for poetry. A poem is a space of encounter, a room of language that invites us to move our senses over its living surfaces, to brush our bodies against its echoes and pressures, visual, sculptural, sonic. A poem refuses to let us be shut down, locked out, cut off — it uses language to frame a gate to experience, calls our bodies to enter. Nothing human is off limits, no experience beyond its horizon: everything we hold is welcome in a poem's meeting place of sound.

Its thresholds shiver with aliveness, its textures with intimacy. It's pluralistic, participatory. A poem shares its breath, presses forward for you, forehead and fingerprints, ushers you across vast distances, to lay the weight of your living skin against its own, knowing the translated state that elicits: the miracle of transmission, connection, communion, exchange.

When you read a poem, you mingle with it — it's a third-degree transfer, subcutaneous. To lift from Janet Frame, when you enter a poem you are re-entering the human voice, the ribs it once hollowed, the throat it drew taut, the palate it rippled, the teeth it insisted against — it asks you to use your mouth to raise the words from its chest, grant them fresh harbour in yours.

A poem's presence opens and moulds to us, mouth, hands, memory, empathy, musculature, heart. It sanctions leaning in, it solicits lingering, it licenses touch, inhalation, taste — and it wants to leave a residue, an afterburn, the scent of its intentions, the pulse of its tissues, the trail of its tongue and its secrets, the brimming of its yesterdays, the burden of its scars.

Even if what it sometimes calls us closer to witness is the tolling of remoteness, loneliness — perhaps a flatline vista (as in Tessa Keenan's 'Ōākura Beach') where 'extinction / is the only thing' on the shore — a poem is populated, its cold sands resonant, its shadows animated, playing on the edge-dwelling voice, the urge to speak which still drags its stick along the coast to scrape out some trace of self.

'Sometimes you have to go in the heart alone', as the child says prophetically in Leah Dodd's piece, clambering through the museum's fake heart-cavity, but such is the paradox of poetry that even this stinky exhibited plastic organ can raise an image of indelible love as we sit with the speaker to contemplate the contemporary planet-wide mess from the 'allocated black bench' of adulthood.

Whatever bittersweet shreds we can scrape from the carcass are enough, more precious for their shimmering scarcity. Even in sharing the deadweight of isolation, the stillpoint of mortal frailty, a poem somehow restocks our senses with shape and graze, the play of light and mind, whisper and fingertip, motion, longing and utterance.

The poems in this remarkable issue will call you to enter scene after scene: 'a haven / a shithole / a murder scene / . . . an edible garden / . . . a site of pilgrimage / a meeting ground.' It may be a space bathed in reverie or blooded with history, a shelter woven from ancestors' softnesses or nailed from stark forbidding boards, a shoreline that stretches in fathomless glittering or slides wasteladen to industrialised gulf, a cityscape glinting with electric galleries or towering with multi-storeyed poverties. But whatever direction it takes you, it urges you to cross whole, to witness 'the sheets and the piss / . . . and the spit and the sweat / and the semen and whenua blood', to feel what the speaker, and even their forebears, knew, felt, suffered, lost, praised, decried, broke through, withstood, held sacred, loved, set light to, 'in that place between the cross / and the chimney, above the buttercups, over the river', among these spaces of resistance and resilience, amid these rooms.

You'll see that we've re-titled this annual collection of spaces *Poetry Aotearoa* — a name-strengthening, a name-deepening, a fuller sounding of the same encounter; a call to the closer voicing and sharing of who, at our kaleidoscopic but tightly interwoven core, we really are.

Tracey Slaughter
November 2022

Competition winners

This year's *Poetry Aotearoa Yearbook* is pleased to publish the winning poems in its annual *Poetry Aotearoa Yearbook* Student Poetry Competition.

'William II' by Jayne Ault (Wellington Girls' College) appears on page 54; 'Medusa' by Hannah Wilson (Raphael House Rudolf Steiner School) on page 198; and 'Aged' by Chantelle Xiong (St Andrew's College) on page 209.

Featured Poet

Tyla Harry Bidois

OUROBOROS

TEETH

i.

there has to be a tooth somewhere — inside the words,
a sharpness;
if i can't love you without hurting you, would i live in you
like a wound; something you tend under the bandage of
your rib that throbs;
the part of romance that is
the longest dusk and throne — pain infinite as moonlight,
systems amassed of breaking as all supernovas
a cloister of many tiny deaths.

ii.

hope like a fever, an unreasonable illness,
incurable; i am back to hiding it inside
my skeleton again, inventing crooks for
these small, foolish allowances.

iii.

breaking; perhaps the most beautiful word,
breaking; to break; to be broken;
his mouth broke against mine the value of fire,
his hands break against my hands the injury
and cure of what skin amounts, the heart
without a name;
& the heart — rapture — breaking;
this, the first house and coffin of grief,
of love, of god.

CANNIBAL LOVE-SONG

i.

his eyes were on the scythe; how much it was shaped like a mouth,
kissing wheat goodnight as though a thousand, half-sleeping
orphans.
that is the way to end things, with the red blade of a kiss.

ii.

dark compliments; you have used eros' arrows as toothpicks,
snapped their bones inside your jaw, the full taste of the organ
alive on your tongue like sap — you sleep the sunlight
out of the skin, one weeping bloodstain of dark;
fishbowl of a world, heaven has been sacked,
apple-trees on fire,
punctured fruit crimson as curdled veins —
you must imagine paradise as match-lit rose,
perfection wilting into gold;
immolation that is nearly a swoon;
something unbearable;
you have fed me the awful words,
many syllabic murders — there is always,
there is forever, and there is never,
never, never,
the knife in my hand and chest.

iii.

scar tissue, the way it shines; the frozen lake
of the skin,
little moon hidden in you.

iv.

the black sweatshirt that contains the shiver,
sweat-laden; modern life;
i am angry,

bleeding eternity out of you,
the technologies you made me use
to clog the flood — watch, my mouth
around plastic, chirping fish. i am addicted
to my own murderer; so much him,
i have injected into my skin a promise
to his machine.

v.

but when i eat your heart, you will hate me.
but when i eat your heart bloody, and the valve explodes
into my throat as though it were a small
and fragile star;
cannibal love-song, you will hate me.

vi.

i.

there's an aftertaste — something in your mind
that lingers like a stain.
substantial, the agony you've tolerated
into desire. you will search for it again
all your life.

ii.

how glorious, a soul; tender preciousness,
terrible secret i protect between
the rib and the wool, the cotton, the silk;
in nakedness, i hide you
in pale, the gentle humiliations of a body,
whatever womanly line and curse
there is, the claw
inside the breast;
i wonder how you would burn.

iii.

cruelty is a stem, a creature that can
flower; i don't know where you come from
until you crawl into my bed
with a new mask, a new skin slick
with story —
the great shape-shift,
even you adore most where you aren't
found; our fondest joke,
alien-thing, intruder;
alone at last, you would calcify.

iv.

because. this, explanation. this,
causation. i want to rip you, the ocean apart,
with it — i want it to be the only purpose,
reason for love-make, the nether-wound
it leaves behind.

vii.

yes, fall headfirst into hurt;
this is the way i like you, strong inside the injury,
it is the only manner of knowing you are human.
of the first well-spring.
we are born weeping; pain is our first language,
the meeting place; amputate yourself from this
and you are already dead — you feed on me
feeding on you, this current of sickness
and cure that sprouts bright
and dreadful as tears —
even stars collapse.

viii.

to hands, touch is prayer; to a mouth then,
speech is ladder to god — song, a thousand doves.
we are transparent animals, primitive,
everywhere we architect
whispers to who we are; the absence
of ourselves is madness, its remedy creation.
i remake the tower, the tiny prison cell, the university
dormitory;
i reshape it all into myself — even you.
the liars we are in confessing we don't want
it all beautiful, the agonising kind of perfect,
the liars we are, lost in our own eyes,
holes only the pretty artefact mends,
flawless and without a soul.
be a mannequin with me, marble
and cold.

ix.

banknote of a life, though the price is steep;
fearful economy, this expensive flesh.
i watch my tear-ducts produce a waterfall,
my diamonds, swear this is how
the man does make me pay.

x.

time is a ruin — though i want it all
regurgitated neatly inside my hands, but i want it all
saturated inside my molars, but i want it all
syrup inside my guts, but i want it all
wallowed and decayed around my fingers,
but i want it all bleeding as i bleed,
dying when i die —
in this, the both of us are selfish,
the sickness, the thirst of thirsts.

KELLY

numb to the lap-dance. the body's million open mouths,
the pink-saliva and crash of it;
as being near you is one seduction all the same,
and by your right of what control is, i expel you so
in parts that we are insects to each other.
and fuck, what power there is in such a desex,
i think that i stare eye-to-eye with god.

BOYS ON CRACK

i.

the rose is the garden's greatest metaphor; it is all beauty and its
suffering.

ii.

methamphetamine in the bathtub; is this what your tears are made of?
you have turned everything into a narcotic. i am a freckle floating
in a pipe, the silhouette of soot in a decapitated lightbulb,
the fire and gasoline of lighter singes
into me the day.
crystalline stain of a smile into your smile,
is this where happiness lives? a breath, an hour,
an afternoon of glorious stupor, only you and the rain, only
you and the divine abyss of your instrument, sooted,
the coal and sleep in your tonsils;
is this where happiness lives? is that where it escapes to,
and so, is that why i haven't found it?
the two of us severed from each other by the chemical's knife,
scissor, the tinfoil of your teeth in the dark
where i'm not.
recognising the unbelonging of yourself
making flaw like love
into my soul.

iii.

the cigarette that makes the hand into a pair of pliers.
only the fire and the kiss bruise the chest on purpose,
as all life is — the fire, the kiss.

iv.

you are an antagonism, an intruder.
the same as a leech, a small and benign cancer.
you hurt in the way of nuisances, cruel
and common snickers,
hiding the thorn inside consistence,
the everyday of me that you drive into your life.
you will let me go, or you will not have limbs;
you will go laughing, spitting,
howling the monster of my figure
into the moon, the morning
stars,
the great joke you have bitten your nails
into; who will you be without me?

v.

i will shake you out of art; all the wombs
i slipped from. i want you delirious,
enamoured, dying without me. i want you
in hell — married to irons,
the black python of night about you,
sweet the nectar of coma —
you of the black touch, tainted me
of light; look here,
i sound like you, look here,
my butterflies, gathered around
feathered bone of their mouths
where, in haste, like all else, is prolonged
thirst; seed of want, but where are you?
i have become the wood, its horrible neutrality
essential as roots.

IT IS MIDNIGHT AND I HAVE HORNS

cardiac chamber — awful, consummate
oyster shell and fist of the chest; the ever-organ,
red lake with all its drowning,
baptised in its yolk (good heart, i am a valve,
                                        a million working veins)
though all this time is an accumulation of denials;
no, i am not this wretched bloodlet, these pines,
claret longing in the throat, the hands,
no, i am not the standing coffin, the cadaver animate,
i am not the heart-attack of the gaze, burst artery of tears,
the unspeakable clot between two bodies.

DARLING

i.

the feeling you have left with god. your invention of him,
always the wrath, the drinking, the belt-whip of your father.
we were always divided by two crosses; there,
in the sanctuary where you have assembled court,
paranoid and in search of lies.
your cleansing is a punishment; a punishment;
being near you is such a heaven, it can't exist
until we die.

ii.

how did i get here? this, the longest post in a series
of incredulous days; the end of a beaten path
veered into by accident, answerless,
there is only that i was normal once,
fell through the void in my sleep
caught the strange in the hook
of my smile;
i have sawed into the mirror since,
played into my cheeks like a violin.
did you know the body is comprised
of strings?

iii.

the empty sensation you have nursed.
you love this: your eyes, half-moons, drowsed
in guilt and the agony lacerated into yourself,
deep in love,
the romance of regret that strips
you of being a whole man;

lets you flounce a while, waif-like and vulnerable,
victim to your own longing stark
as summertime;
you shine inside your pain,
bright as stars.
i watch you drink into yourself startled with it.

iv.

you are blind; greater than any faith,
any breast or thigh that is your road-map into hell.
somehow, i think this is sternest commitment
in your blood; your sweat;
where you are all fluid, bartering.

v.

i hate it when he calls me '*darling*'. the south
is there, certainly, but more the crocodile
than the willow. how do you endear yourself
to something so cold adept to such a heat?
the mistrust sits in the voice, hisses
along the wheat-field of the tongue
into the air.

vi.

have no time for the stupidity that harms. though i like
to laugh, and what silliness it is, those clapping lungs,
so much nothing; the light, the light;
i think it injures monsters, this sound,
the amulet of a mouth,
i think it purges rooms.

vii.

the compelling aspects of storms;
violence as only violence is, and so it cleanses;
there is no villain in it. hurt as only hurt,
as only chaos, as only the wild teardrop
of life; you are only hating a void,
the earth without conscience.

viii.

go away.

ix.

they come to you with secrets, these protective
women, aware of another man's sanctity;
they come to you all teeth, loathing that is its
own confession, the first women-speak,
a creature we learned in school, hiding
from men ourselves into the handkerchief
of something closer to a sister.
though i speak your language, woman,
hear inside its jaws the small abuses
of a heart;
unflattering, unbelonging and raw.

x.

when we are trapped on a rowboat.
one snarl snapped in two,
stabbing the quiet of your eyes.
and whatever cupids sung before
singe into the gasoline of our breath
crisp as fresh matches.

such a distance — almost familial,
we will set the lake on fire.

xi.

such day, the broken fork of light
through the wrists of greyest foams; such
wind, ultimate conductor, restless and causeless
dance; such skin, all of us the red kiss of a silent
church, a cascading bruise of living amount
upon each other; such sound, the rose-petals
of mouths and echoed prayer of lungs
shaped and contained as pink leaves —
(are you a flower?) — such fire,
first flesh-eater, its enormous appetite
of forgiving and bright, bright,
bright, the fingerprint
of god; such water, everything
punctured that bleeds, saps, melts,
everything that drains itself into the tears
of heaven,
too divine for temple; (i will pray
for you); such heart, rhythmic inflation
in the wolf's throat that is the small
star's drum, the moon-song,
the ballad of all beasts.

xii.

though he is still the scratch, unhealed matter
    beneath the thin scab of the chest.
    it splits awake the lid of a jewellery
    box, copper wire,
    all of the machine's lead in song,
    the fluttering, mechanical wing

that crying is,
subdued the eerie pivot of a
dull-painted ballerina inside
skin, drilled between the ribs
as any knife.

xiii.

fury, youth; i want all the legends, see,
i want the audacity of golden eras
locked inside the silicone
of my talons; eyes of two fly-traps,
caught the face of whatever long promise
there was to age; i want to sound
like all the dreams dressed in white,
flaxen sunrises and the fair of barricaded
libraries set alight in winter; blonde rome,
i want to be a nightmare,
(the seed of many pointed fingers in a square
when asked, 'whose fault is this?')
i want you to revolve around me
as though i am the sun.

xiv.

i am arrogant; thief of time,
i take words back and snuff them into expense
as though it were a vault;
this, the humble word of only one person,
inopportune joke from a pew;
there is nothing of multitudes about it,
nothing of a warning, a decree, there is nothing
of man's alchemy that is one voice shattered
into mass, returned in particles
as everything made of sky and light;

all this universe that is collapse
and resurgence, the condense
of a long ceremony of frivolous atoms;
everything is the function
of breath; everything is the envelopment
of stars dying, alive;
dying, alive;
we explode into each other.

BYSSHE

i don't think two poets should be in love; this one serpent consuming itself.
the enchantment dies, explodes from overuse and the numbness of two tacticians —
in my life, the seduction of a common defect or talent crawls through fascination and into war;
my song will eat your song. it must. it's too much blood. i'd hurt you inside it after you have hurt me,
summon his face into it like the petals of my favourite knife. i love hiding behind men,
the way they hurt each other better through the inevitability
of too much nearness;
the curtain of being only a woman is its own weapon there — and aware that i know,
i slip behind and away. what do you know about stolen light?
what do you know about this kind of contagion, this kind of lucency?
how could you love me yet fight me for the same god?

MELPOMENE

i.

melpomene, one mustn't call their face a mask unless they would see
another wear it. you have called yourself a performance,
and often — so i have seen other men pick up the hat and rattle. i
have seen them share your spine; move inside your skin
for the boundary the way reptiles do,
unstitching themselves from their own colours.
i know the spirit as something that can be shed with you,
something artificial when it is heavy or difficult,
learns all your tricks,
wakes to the shame of having wanted it once,
wiser,
suddenly mutating.
you adore into plateau,
into the glorious churning in your chest
that calls you human,
a liar that knew me.
if nowhere else, that will be my
habit, my playground

i made you into my secret name;
i made you into a covenant
i hid into myself,
to abandon you was to light my temple

on fire; losing you was an injury to

the god in me.

ii.

woman-kind are all descended from a kind
of genocide; all descended from beauty,
the sacked village, bodies burning around
her body salvaged by its shape; woman-vein,
this red-lipped hope wifed into the cruel we have lived with, wore
wreaths beside,
the testimony of loving as the circumstance of survival;
the wombs that have been opened
in the solace of this blank stare we pass down like an inheritance, the
dark
gift of our quiet old as the first child; song;
the first sunrise bright as blood.

science says that trauma alters the genome; the violences
are flower-bulbs of a bouquet we collect as a family;
woman, though you are feast after the confirmation
of your foremother's rape to some steel-made chiefdom,
though you are so many houses alight; the spilled wine
from the smashed glass of his throat; though you are so
many confusions, the internal fingers pondering the source
of a nostalgic hurt, something between your skin and the
shadow, something between your skin and the moonlight,
everywhere you've bled, older than dread, its first teardrop.

iii.

what did we give up when we agreed to these men?
i look for myself and i am always in parts; woman-sky,
woman-moon, woman-earth and all its volcanic romances;
they sutured us so carefully from the root; in man's sprouting into
oneness, we
are all praying to our fathers, manufacturing him as face of the divine.
though

this is my son's face,
what my gut architects; though he looks at me, and sees an
appendage, a
dismembered part of his body that builds him altars,
keeps his stomach warm, weeps at his crucifixion, observes his
courage into the
parting of the sea that had my name once, though where he goes this
becomes the
secret we both forget and have forgotten;
though my pondering is made sacred by his tolerance of what i am,
blanket-
maker, family-cook, bed-warmer,
though his tolerance is machinated by what we left in time, old
pantheon, the many
seers,
shadows numerous and articulate as stars.

iv.

i compared you to the sky to begin with.
i must remember: the t-shirt, ripped in places;
the coffee-stained tabletop,
your hand and its small scar, some forgotten scrape along your
transit to my frame — your lip, its judgemental
constitution, how it puckers
when you are snickering, and there is a part of you that enjoys the
funeral of everything that dictates its obstruction; your hair, the dry
ends, the soap that smells of cheap vanilla; thirty years of toothpaste,
and you still can't contain the froth inside your mouth; like me, it
bleeds.

WINGED AND IN THE DARK

i.

it is not possession, because i am always there; though half-lidded and curiously drained,
i swear there may be a wraith that sings through me an instrument,
and i swear heaven sounds only like another broken heart escaping itself.
a host no less prime a moonstruck girl that tantrums and crawls back
home, apologies in her wrists and thighs —
'darling, please forget the nights i broke the door,
and was entombed again
to another ancient thing, two black eyes and a leash;
darling, she was only another dungeon, i was snuffed
like a candle — suddenly, i was homesick.'

ii.

courage, man; the wilderness was your house first,
cities and certainty have plundered the lions out of you.
guitars scream, primitive, and you smash them into the stage
for it, tenderest reply,
and i think,
this is what your soul sounds like, something
you punish for its barbarism that you
keep locked in the bone jar of your body;
here is your midnight, finding hard floors,
gutters, the angular
sleeping places to shard into.

iii.

be wary, always;
through joint integrities, they will force the door open
and close it once their men are inside,
without the steadfast jaw of your hunger open and unsatisfied,
that will be closure of your movement;
dictation from the clouds that change shape, hue,
but a rain the same make and purpose;
harvest everything,
break the shackles open even when they have been learned
into your lovers;
breaking is a kind of loving,
it educates your burden off the dinner table, out of
the bed, off their skin and oil that you suckle
dry.
discover your sweetheart like a reckoning, a divine injury;
the arrow in their shoulder.

iv.

with the coldness of a mountain, teach me how to
take care of your heart;
as there are men who want snow
in whatever they do, when and how should i
reserve from you, the sunrise? the dark sun behind
my eyes —
the pomegranate slid apart is doppelgänger
to the open cavity of the chest; tender seeds,
red capsules of a dream, how do i keep you sweet
inside your sleeping?
i circle you like your bones.

v.

there is an art to it — to be together and alone;
    fight the hive-mind like a curse, an illness. always
exorcised to innumerability
    though we have been made so similar; two eyes and cheeks,
    the sunflower of a mouth that speaks the same words
    on occasion;
    though two emeralds form in the same cave, birthed the same
    calamity of rock and pressure — avoid, with me, the carver,
    our smile the saddest twinship from their clavicle
    and that forever there, weeping in light;
        i want to be the thing that cuts — that is survival.

vi.

as opulence — yes, that is the word — the decadence
of a meaning, even at its dimmest point a black glamour
about it;
that is how we must know each other, wherever we meet
in the deprivation of ourselves,
two moths in the shadow;
see how these small creatures dance, winged
and in the dark.

THYSANIA or THE BURDEN OF FLOWERS

i.

when the body is young, is supple, is breast, is smooth,
    is rouge, is lean,
the mouth forms about the poem
so sprite in sex,
it dives from the tongue upon the open sheet
of all becoming loud — how could we ever be clean?
the porcelain of sound that, in your ear, sordid just the same
as mine — alight me in your mind the red phlegm of bodies,
then. the caveman's first sign language surged as a torch

ii.

i have cut into the garden of my stomach,
to look for you, i suppose,
    secret-bone, other-heart; on nights like
    these, i tear, like book-pages, your residues
    from myself,
    the soft-leather of my body closes quiet,
    empty into the morning, blood-red
    against the mountains,
    furious.

An interview with Tyla Harry Bidois

The colour red soaks this selection from featured poet Tyla Harry Bidois, dripping its sensuous shade through verse after verse, imbuing lines with richness and violence — a coloration fleshed out by the sonic intensity of her driven spoken tempo (if you've ever had the treat of hearing her read, you feel present at a feast, a divine vocal assault, a fierce rite).

Opulent, raw, incantatory, audacious, surging — the poems of *Ouroboros* pitch themselves directly into the 'open cavity' of the heart, interrogating the 'blood-price' of relationship, setting the seething textures of myth against 'sweat-laden; modern-life'. Here love is a luscious no-exit economy of 'you feed on me feeding on you', the thrall of addiction wrapping its 'black glamour' around a perpetual reckoning. With the 'full taste of the organ / alive on [her] tongue' the speaker of *Ouroboros* stays 'strong inside the injury', wielding the lyric image-energies and melodic force that arise from surrender, a creature of 'delirious / enamoured' rhythms who chants directly into the face of tragedy, drinking the pain of self-destructive love with a red-rinsed smile, fighting always to live.

Tracey Slaughter: Sheer vocal energy is probably the first thing that strikes the listener or reader of your work — your poems always thrum with insistent bodily beats. Where did your unshakeable sense of voice arise from — is it instinctive, inherited or both? How much was it influenced by spoken word or oral traditions?

That's such a wonderful compliment and thank you so much. I'm deeply inspired by oral traditions, spaces where poetic verse began without need of or accessibility to paper. The Pacific knows this intimately, as well as the ancient Greeks, the Romans, the Vikings. There's something about it that cuts through the classism that has existed in publishing and business where parties have shunned the political poet into corners of art where their stories had to be heard instead of read — and of course, that gave way to the importance of self-publishing, spoken word and zine culture. It's punk rock, it's cultural impact against constructs that have barred certain people from higher education and the privilege of owning books, and it's a tradition old as time.

I think I first became aware of it in my introduction to Shakespeare, who was writing for performance in arenas where the audience may not have necessarily been literate but were nevertheless welcome to judge for themselves the validity and beauty of his work. The same for the early Greek playwrights. The awareness of the relationship between poetry and sound is very much an active part of my mind when I'm writing, even for the page, and I suspect that's a mixture of both an instinctive preference as well as an inherited one. I'm very proud to be a part of the spoken word tradition. As someone of mixed race — which includes Asian, Italian, Greek, Scandinavian and Indigenous (Te Arawa Māori and Cherokee) heritage — I love the idea of contributing to a grand practice of storytelling that connects me to the writing and performance culture of today as well as what was developed by my ancestors, and the ancestors of anyone who would likely read or hear my work.

TS: Mythic themes and patterns always seem to pulse in your work, too, recasting contemporary settings and experiences in auras of the underworld, unconscious and ancient. How deliberate is this invocation of myth throughout your writing — or does it just erupt unbidden? When did you first find yourself drawn to its motifs and textures?

I think there may have been a time where I wasn't drawn to myths and legends, but that was probably between my mother's second and third trimester! To me, the exploration of myth being intrinsically attached to poetry comes from the role of the poet as myth-maker and storyteller. And of course, if you read enough poetry, and especially the Greeks, you'll find that nearly every poet turns into Orpheus. We become skilled so as to be able to enter certain rooms of consciousness precisely as he did, with the hope that if we are very good and worthy in this pursuit, we too might be able to leave Hades unharmed. Across religious denominations, when we return to this house, we all worship the spring. We are all Orpheus. And we still have that awful, niggling flaw of needing to look back — but isn't that the poet's job? I think a lot of poets (and musicians) romanticise myth with a sense of recognising themselves in the compulsion to tell stories, and tell stories beautifully.

TS: *Ouroboros* unleashes images of myth to explore the subject of relationships — couples caught in intimate, fatalistic deadlock, bound into standoffs of unrelenting love, feel at its core. How crucial is the appeal to an other, an urgently faced or confronted 'you', to your poems? Do the provocations or antagonisms of connection often motivate your work?

Poetry is one of the best places to explore the impact and potential of human connection, absolutely. Although poetry written for the sake of exploring beauty in verse has great merit, it's the way that language is able to express intimacy between two living things that breathes life into the work. My favourite poets confront romance as well as the inevitable falling away from relationships and people that one encounters as time passes. I think the point of the poet and the artist is to isolate particles of moments that matter most, whether painful or tragic.

TS: Addiction is another of the bodily dramas which seem central to *Ouroboros* — your dissection of codependent ruin and dead-end chemical craving feels acute. How important, and how challenging, was it to explore this theme in your work?

It was extremely important and challenging — our current technological environment has provided such an interesting arena for fast love and fast hatred. And it can be so dark sometimes, and entirely by accident, this daily onslaught of sex and politick that the mind has been conditioned into absorbing. My subjects tend to be in the middle of conflict and movement, whether that's through exposure to temptation to drugs or ill decision in love, because so much of my scope has been shaped by relationships with people going through issues along with me going through mine — and many of them have had problems with addiction. The tightrope to walk is in being able to develop that narrative in writing honestly, as well as taking care of the reader's emotional welfare. Confronting things is wonderful and the artist's right, but without room for catharsis, it changes the poem from a place of solace to a place to be subjected to abuse.

TS: Your poetry, from the moment I first heard it, struck me as pouring from a deep personal source. What subjects are currently driving you? What's next for your poetry?

As an Italian with an obvious obsession for drawing allegories between antiquity and modern-day, I hope to continue developing my written voice in areas of myth and legend. I think it's exciting to place the modern tone in places it doesn't seem to fit at times and find ways to make it work. I'm currently working on my third collection, which will delve into fairy tales with an adult spin that should hopefully bring new insight and ideas to chronicling the sensation of growing up in verse, as well as a project centred on the Oracle of Delphi. And thank you to *Poetry Aotearoa Yearbook* for allowing me the opportunity to discuss this. Thank you so much, and god bless.

New Poems

Pip Alfeld

The Roofer

Sealed well, no salted water meets me
But we can hear him, one bootlace untied
And crying on our tin roof

Necks flexed and throats offered
Salutes shielding the sun, we gaze up

Can he see us down here, or hear us up there
Perspectively small, he pictures us all taller

'Too high for us' someone says
His gaze mesmerised by something
Absent from our line of sight
Reverting to slouches defeated
By the view he's addicted to

With so much on his plate
I'll be his smoko for a small time
She'll be his weekend and he'll be his
Recovery

'You're an artist'
I call up to him, from beneath this crafted shelter
Though enough
Though galvanised
He still knows
Salt this roof and it will rust

Relapse into kinship
Need me
Just stay this way longer

Or don’t.
We’ll return again all the same
To be looked upon and never down on
Occupying not his shadow
His shade
To imagine us taller is to
See ourselves through the roofer’s eyes

John Allison

How to sing sunlight

Look at the light dancing on the waves
    I say to Martha. She is five years old.
Sunlight is so hard to catch, she says
    but it catches everything in the whole

wide world. She sings a song. I ask her
    if she has learned it at kindergarten.
I'm making it up just now, she says
    it's what the sun is singing to the sea.

And runs off dancing her songlines
    of the sun and sky and wind and sea
elated all the way across the sand
    into the open arms of everything . . .

Invasive weeds, or I wish I could give you the world but I was only given mud, rot and the bones of a half-eaten fish

for my seven-week-old child

First swim after they cut me open. The mud tried to smother the sand stolen from the other side of the country to build the fake beach. There are no fish. Pipes are spurting waste water into the harbour. Once a volcano here that erupted and shaped this body of water. I often want to hold water in my hand, as if it was measured in weight rather than volume. Slippery and slimy. Invasive weeds. In Europe all the water is brown. Many bodies have floated in those waters both alive and dead. Some were sold, some were stolen, some were just poor, some had no other options. In summer the water drowns so many here, as the sun gets hotter and the threat of fires loom, but the tuna started returning to the lakes and the rivers, despite the trout that don't belong there taking all the food. When my waters broke the mucus was brown and it almost choked my baby floating inside my body. The baby didn't want to leave and arrived in a sterile grey factory with twenty people in blue aprons watching, while David Bowie played. The surgeon's incision. King of the goblins please take this baby somewhere safe. Who can blame you though for not wanting to leave the womb? I wish I could give you the world but I was only given mud, rot and the bones of a half-eaten fish.

Land back but not written on earrings and sold online. Sea spray. Land back as praxis not practice. The labour required to fix it or to not fix any of it. What are the consequences for the vulgarity and materialism of this colonial barbarism? Or rather its dredges? Invasive weeds. Native weeds. Native title. Hands that can never be clean. Washing the sheets. Soaking the nappies. Land back as in for this tiny baby. Land back as in not just the restitution of the land, or the power to make decisions, but the water, the birds and all of our kin. Not ownership in a 'legal' land title way. Land back as in a rejection of corporate structures. Land back as in new knowledge meets old knowledge and not repeating the same mistakes. Land back as in no more mimicry. Land back as a futurity that includes self-determination, environmental sustainability, and economic justice. I wish I could give you the world but I was only given mud, rot and the bones of a half-eaten fish.

Hair spreads out like lumps of seaweed smashing against the rocks. Sea fog. Knife darts between fingers. Slime. Invasive weeds. The sandbags are breaking. The mounds are collapsing as the water licks the feet. Purebred dogs. The sea reclaims the shore. Breast milk leaking. Clothes latch to the chest of salt and sweat. Let-down reflex. My body senses babies to feed. Not my own, but all others. Bodies and the endless cycle of hunger. Something about staying still and never forgetting. Wetting the bed. Changing nappies. Relaxing too much in the sauna. Becoming only liquid. It's hard to hold anything 'in this economy'. Sea spray. Rata flower. Ice cream scream. FONTERR(OR) dairy products. Backbone of the nation state. Pour animal fat down the drain. Body made of algae from the river. Viruses are the most numerous biological entities on earth. I can't breathe in this mask even after seven, eight, nine booster shots. I'll take them all if it'll keep you safe. When most of a continent has had only one shot if any. Borders. Restrictions. Wanting a slice of the pie and a seat at the table. Variants fly out old and new trade routes. Paranoia. Distrust that's an old open wound. Red, blue and green pills. Swallow them all. I wish I could give you the world but I was only given mud, rot and the bones of a half-eaten fish.

Children's playgrounds become dog parks. No shitstains on your white shoes. 'Upward mobility' and home ownership. Inflation. Swan carcass in the reservoir. Invasive weeds. Protected species. Gamey meat between two slices of white bread. Not butter but margarine. Tomato sauce. Manaakitanga. Sucking marrow from the bones. Suckling the hands in search of the breast. A whole lemon pushed into every orifice. Eating the plums off of the tree. The excess rots into the soil flowering more trees and more plums. The causality of change. Plants grow through the concrete and around the steel. Let's rebuild but never erase. I wish I could give you the world but I was only given mud, rot and the bones of a half-eaten fish.

Ruuaumoko shakes like a screaming child awake for twelve hours, wide eyed and overtired. Squirming but still asleep on my chest. Searching for a feed. Dreaming but what to dream of. The cathedral is covered in plants again. All buildings reclaimed. Invasive weeds. It's less simple and more rapid than before. The ice melts and the swamps become farms again and again and again. Kūmara mounds remain. Dug into the hills by hand. Elevator up to the sky. Sea spray. Cows over hands shitting in the volcanic soil. Productive. Fertile. Milk production saps. Babies aren't born anymore. They are ripped out. Pain erupts, but my pain hides another's pain who hides another's pain and so forth. It's hidden deep in my body. Buried but growing. I wish I could give you the world but I was only given mud, rot and the bones of a half-eaten fish.

Fossilised microorganisms. Invasive weeds. Before there were the oceans. Deep in the biosphere in hyperthermal vents. A collective memory. A shift. Nothing remains shut. There are no holidays, no breaks, no pauses. No secrets can stay hidden. Every story is remembered differently but the soil knows the truth. The past is a scar on the land. It never completely heals, but the cut appears superficial and closed until it opens again. I wish I could give you the world but I was only given mud, rot and the bones of a half-eaten fish.

Sylvia

We should've known, I'm just
Another poet come to bite your face off.
Another blood moon teenager, craning
    To catch something beautiful. A
    Midnight haircut, lonely curl dead
    In your hand. Another gothic shape
Tarring your horizon, dark omen
In the dregs of your tea. One final
Prayer in your ear on the carpet,
    Saying, *how simple to predict that you*
    Would make this all about yourself.
    Quite selfish to love in secret
Rather than loudly and with
Insidious intent. This room feels
Of sureness, which opens us out
    Into a place of constant rivers.
    A place of grey light and water
    And other people, and I can't quite
Reach where I am meant
To be going. I can't find my mouth,
Just your cheek in the darkness.

Jane Arthur

The Sky is Bigger

If we drive slightly past our place, the hills become
bare of houses, filled with trees in every shade of dark green
like stepping back in time. The sky is bigger.
The distance is hazier. The birds are more rare,
and enormous and full of pluck. We have different ideas
about what makes good driving music, so we usually turn it
right down and talk instead. We both hate driving. Me because
I do it and you because you can't. We tag-team bad moods, which
is my latest, most appreciative definition of romance.
Every day I point at something and ask how long
has that been there and you always say forever.

William II

01.05.22

It came back, but like you said over breakfast, 2 a.m. cereal, it always does
You shared your (favourite) overly expensive box and we sat
with heavy eyelids in your kitchen
I said everything I had been scared to say for months
You whispered wisdom and I began to wonder how someone so
comforting could be so sad
How have we lasted this long?

Weirdly, I couldn't imagine anything bad possibly happening in this
house, but every house
has a deep enough sadness if you just wait for the sun to go down
Your sink was too clean, like you were trying to bleach the blood out
of it
Your bed was a brick against my back, as though you haven't broken
into it yet, spending so
many nights away from home
Tell me what you're running from, and I'll do what I always do and grip
your hands and
wonder how you have the patience to sustain long nails for as long as
you have

Driven past the station at 10 p.m., singing like an idiot in the car while
you two argued in the
front seat like a married couple
After he's gone home you tell me why you were crying that one night
and despite myself I
start laughing
That's why I was crying, too, I tell you
I'm glad we both survived

spaces fill silver

bright white highlights
the spaces in our brains
pools in vertebral bodies
labral tears swollen bursae
fills the wells in lungs and breasts
shines through holes in fat and bone

our pockets of water
silver coins pressing on
nerves thoughts veins
squeezing out pins
needles poems dry
shouts in the dark

we wait in white rooms watch
spaces fill silver on a screen
wonder what we had to lose
to make room for these holes
what fell clinking with our keys
leaving space the shape of shining coins

'appendicitis'

when I was 12 I had my appendix out
and I didn't have appendicitis.
dad smuggled my bunny into the hospital
hid her in an antique doctor's bag
she didn't mind — must have found it like a burrow
I don't remember holding her
just the outline of
an ammonite moment
impressed.

I'd faked it, though I wasn't sure why
life's too hard to diagnose
better to transubstantiate
can you count down from ten for me?
ten nine eight seven
part of the blameless ether.

when I woke up the seconds collided
split time down the middle
minutes popped like rock candy
a drip fed me morphine and
the hours trickled through me.

I was there a while — a bad reaction to the gas
belly distended stomach jammed
morphine to melt the pain
melt the curtains and the nurses
(who were so like friends)

and every day I hurt was a good day
another day away
until mum had to go home and shower;
dad could stay with me that night.

my breath got clogged — eyes were beestings — swollen guts spilled out
monitors alerted;
mum showered at the hospital
and the next day
when he brought my bunny in an antique doctor's bag
I thought: *how silly.*

Tony Beyer

L'addition

there are days at my age
when contemporaries' miseries
seem to accumulate
and close out the light

a colleague entering the labyrinth
of Alzheimer's
a brother whose scan may reveal
more than any of us bargained for

news of a former near-rival
lugged off to a home for the infirm
where he can literally
dribble in his broth

in other words I suppose
we are having to front up
the boys of summer
beginning winter now

and good for it too I hope
neither whining nor diminishing it by demanding more
of this world we pass on
where having been just once is miraculous

Victor Billot

Your move, again

You asked to meet me by the sea.
Your move. I had already invited you
to the cafe with its eccentric furniture.
Grey light. I walk across dunes
to where you wait on the sand.
The wind hurtles at us and then
rain. Back in the safety of the car
you ask for a kiss. Your move, again.
In amongst the cold and salt,
voltage dances. You pull back.
Surprise in your eyes.
Not mine. I already know.

Hard to reach

from 'For Alyson'

My sister's driving her SUV up and down the rural road
and won't come in. Driving up, I've said, *This alpha shit
it has to stop,* and now she's cross. Inside, our cousin
Alyson, she's dead. Beside the coffin, her grandson says,
My dad plays rugby he used to be a boxer.
I've learnt Alyson followed QAnon,
how deep a fear of hospitals, doctors, it can go.
She took you to her heart till now it's given out.
There's a kind of family whitewash, how we've let
some fall away. The Polynesian-looking ones.
Her fella's in the kitchen, can't say a word.
I go back to the road looking for my sister,
her jeepy thing. She's busy, it's taking time,
to get to be the victim.

Peter Bland

Some places

Some places passed through
over a lifetime
linger like an ache
at dusk. Though rarely
central to the narrative
they tug at the heart
like a lost baroque.
Raw songs once heard
in some ancient street,
paths over a hill
we never took,
old childhood ponds
asleep in the sun . . .
Best let them drift
like the sound of the sea
or arms waving back
from some remembered shore.

Cindy Botha

in the time of fly

which is brief, an indecent
haste

which is a bottle-
green buzz
at the edge
of earshot, sybaritic hum
an aberrant
feasting

which is sucking
from dung, apple-pie
or corpse
nothing off-
limits
touch down to tickle
eyelid, knuckle
thigh

which is gluttonous coupling
brittle lullaby
fitful
as static

which is a wriggling wreath
of maggots
meat running red
on a plate

Iain Britton

This Woman of Honeycombs . . .

& concupiscent dreams

lives

amongst beehives — paddocks of livestock

fenced wooden houses

she contemplates what it costs to look at the rising seas
where people
flop about in waves — who surf the tides
where expressions — collide

*

she likes the sunlight the taste of wild honey
she likes sharing surreal thoughts

& while the world makes seasonal adjustments

she talks of riding the burnt-pink sky
of reading the calligraphic scrapings
of a woman's battle to be someone else

she claims she fits perfectly

into her father's shadow

Mute

Speaking is something,
when you think about it,
like an act of magic:
settling on the surest note
in the mind's skein of keys,
turning sights into sounds, sense
into sentences, marking
time with breezy flourishes
and undeclared caesurae,
steering the tongue
through the mouth, breathing
in and breathing out.
But you forgot how,
you lost everything.
All those careful considerations,
the heedless motor skills patrolling
proud borders, swatting slights
with tart tongue and eye-wither
(the gentle tasks of kiss & caress);
the whole tender, knotty collage
we christen a personality,
bricked into furious silence.

Owen Bullock

The Microbes

Their music fuses punk & progressive rock. They lash out in phases and don't mind the odd mistake. They change like Bowie or Armatrading. They simulate rain at their gigs — it gets the energy up for everyone. They have the audience sing onstage with them. They improvise — some tracks are 25 minutes. They don't sell merch, except for knitting & embroidery patterns you can make yourself. Like to chat & collect your autograph afterwards. They're national treasures & turned up naked to collect their award. There are 12 in the band — they come and go, so they don't need to break up, just evolve. Their new album, *Ramshackle,* is available for free download to the million people with the lowest carbon footprints.

Danny Bultitude

A Town Between Two Highways

I know the feeling of concrete barriers / on either side of roadbridges
Predicting those thoughts / which creep up the cerebellum / unannounced
I know the sparse and skinny / electrical poles encrusted by lichen and
Those neighbouring vehicles / of petroleum truckers who / did not stop

When passing your town where / a bottle of Yenda is all that calms the bees
While prams lie tipped / abandoned on knucklesplit roadside / overseen by an
Old black labrador sat on his vintage / cushioned armchair that's not for sale
Unlike the pizzas and pies / and unending alcohol flows / which froth and spill

From the commercial hotel that doubles / as the Bottle-O warring against
The six other pubs / and turncoat liquor stores / and the short iron fences
Claiming to protect family homes / from inevitable drivers who'll lose control
With Jack Russells in the back / desperate to join the elderly / in Taylor Park

Wearing virginal shirts never kissed by iron / crumpled around the spaces where
Muscles once bloomed / and movement still whirs / sunburn staining the collars
Clinging to the necks of entire generations / gathered together with collective sight
Suddenly able to recognise / that some trees grow / even taller than the overpass.

in this town

1 we wear gumboot bikinis
holding fast to blocked out
    quads racing
hills
blackbirds fall from the sky to iced
up tents in minus 4
whispered voices
    filmy cold & bourbon
heavy
cinderblock   empties.

2 the bouncer lets us in cuz
they're our friend's-cousin's-sister's-boyfriend's-uncle-twice-
removed &
he likes our   lips
we smoke out the toilets &
    cry
    not to cough get
fucked up slip hot into
1 more drink
hands that feel like
meaning   bar eyes whiskeyed up &
honest   to   the moment
snuffed out in
    shoddy bathroom   stalls
    lockless mirrored lights we
wear our years in glittered minis for
lingering eyes their blood
dried worms   hungry in the
bass.

3 there are no lesbians but
we are all bi-
    curious
swapping bottle-spun saliva
boys step out for
boys but we all stay for girls
take   the   full   time
it isn't cheating   it gets
our boyfriends
    hard   but we
learned kissing doesn't
have to taste like
    cold pie & cigarettes
could be lip   roll   suck
    passionpop cherries
between the sheets &
down   past beach boy racer
amps.

4 we wear gold cheeked luck charms slap
down halls filtered grey the
long leg rafters
pumped   loop dat
shimmy shimmy yah &
raspberry-creatine-shot liver
    pools those
skip   step heel stairs
tat up electro smiles   wield
    daggered flesh to
raise voiced car doors
    round about rise
concrete pupils &

bare skin street lamps   record
    scratch   jump
again.

5 we are peppermint strawberry
stick pulled
dollar shop lip gloss &
my chem sheds at the
end   of the night we fall
down in giggles &   *don'ts*   no one
listens   pulsed   up &
black lit so nobody knows
who to hate the next day when
she says she was raped.

6 we circle roads for
that sense of   moving
sip cooking wine in
  backseat corollas get   high
on chamomile thyme & ocean salts   our
  boyfriends suck us to
marrow & cry
    starfish
we learn to   choke
        moan our hips
we learn
to
stay.

Nathaniel Calhoun

burials

you have a small studio
tucked in the woods
you arrive
to find bird carcasses
already flat and dry
lopped
on the ground
beneath deceiving windows

must everything be
tenderly interred
blessed
with flowers
and kind words?
may anything be
kicked around
chucked by wingtip
into thickets?

if
the first hundred times
you bury
small creatures in the wild
you do so
at depth
with flowers
what does it mean
when you stop
with the flowers
when you stop
trying to plant
something on top

when you put them
shallow enough
that fur or feathers
poke through
after light rain?

-sue

after Chop Suey *by Edward Hopper*

Flapping, unshaped in a squall, I'm asked in —
I'm a mess, half made up —
a jigsaw of jazz and prohibition —
(the illusion of freedom consumption yields?)
tied in time by a cloche hat —

these clean lines keep clean *our* lives —
I am more than my gender green pear —
seeing some of the sign,
(a stain-glass window, no revelations)
is the price of enclosure, reduction —

look, *he's* lost in his own smoke subvocalising —
she's gone too and that is not *her* hand —
her mask is complete —
I am more than their make-up and ventriloquism —
I'm a smudge in a white-washed sky —

I am Sue in this chop-suey — know why?

Ella Cartwright

Ūkaipō

I read about your death today
Te Auparo, your body laid down
and shattered
amongst the tulips
in a clash with Ngare Raumati

Rest assured,
despite your death the
roots spread
below you, through those bulbs
and down into the earth
where they have reached me
here, today.

You should know:
Your sons avenged you.

I learned the word *pakanga*
doing homeschool with my
daughter, and I thought
of the way women curl
around the edges of battlefields
like a question mark, or a
lace collar

Our stories of war are
not the main event —
not like the muskets
or the spears,
not like the patu
dressed with brains and blood

not like the patu
dressed with brains and blood

We are the minutiae,
the garnish;
the romance

We are someone deciding
to write down that it was tulips
you were slain on.

E kui, you were honoured
by your boys.

I think of Helen of Troy,
and I think of you —
necks splitting open
in your name

I picture you dancing
on the battlefield
silver and iridescent
while the men who killed you fell

Terrified in their final
moments, confronted
with your warrior sons three

who could still taste your milk
in the backs of their throats

Cadence Chung

postcard

missing is missing is missing, no
matter what anybody says. the
children, peachy-lipped and sticky,
reaching out for a glass cabinet,
are just as lonely as ancient lovers.
their hands, sticky, against the glass
are tiny prayers. an inscription in
a second-hand book is, at once, an
obituary and a dedication to new
life. every heavy-trodden path
stoops down to accommodate each
gentle footstep on its surface, the
earth moving from our roaming.
you can miss someone you've never
met and long for a time you've
never had. it's the body's way of
dealing with the overflow of dust —
unclogging the tear ducts by crying
it all out. once, a woman wrote about
violets to her lover and the letter
passed through so many hands
that it ended up in the greedy mitts of
poets, always lemon-peel preserving
other people's moments and keeping
them for themselves. once, a man
lifted a baby on his shoulder so her
clay-smeared handprint could be
splashed across the cave wall. once,
two men at Pompeii made love as the
pyroclastic flow surged over them.

once, once, once, we all missed
each other and kept trying to turn
so we could see each other's faces,
but time got in the way.

My girl

The favourite / The following / An Anchor /
Dissolving / The Family / The Criteria / My Girl / My Girl / My Girl/
Talking bout / my heart / burn / down / draft / Waking up to / My Girl

//

I got so much
/ envy / My girl / not needing / not starting / not needling / the
stranding / dissolving /
standing off / sure /
/ I love you /

//

Keeping it / again / The Holiday / / honey /
You can't / what can make me / feel / in the box / high / light /

/ what might / that look / like / / my
girl /

//

Month of May /

Fine Family / Floating / toward / un / interested / in / that line /
towards / questions
/ alone / in rooms

/ Full /

//

/ Trolley stacked in bending lines / got sunshine /

on a / cold

outside /

I'd

guess /

Well / might / look like

/ My girl

/ what can make me feel / this way /

On a cloudy day /

She Is a Current of the Dying

She is currently dying between violets and cigarette ash. In the summer humidity of cooing mothers. She is currently dying between lunch box talks and coriander. She is currently dying with her face plastered in La Mer.

She walks dying between rouge lipstick and blistering waistlines. She walks dying between payment penny dreadfuls on show at café Lafayette and the Spoodle's twirl. In-between cobbled streets pecked by Louboutins. She walks dying with a 6-month pregnant belly. Swollen with gas trapped in her intestinal tract.

She lies dying between little girls screaming at their brothers for cutting their barbie's plastic hair. Dogs barking. Weeds gnawing pavements. The Chase reruns. She lies dying. She lies dying.

She died looking at her bookshelf. While I grabbed her a glass of water she didn't need.

This poem plays on Tracey Slaughter's poem 'she is currently living'. Images and lines in 'she is currently living' inevitably led to this poem.

would you like to lay down?

would you like to lay down?
careful on the mattress like a flame
flickering in the casting of your light
with a pop and crackle you warm me

the estuary of your body is lithe and waiting
curled below, beyond, and forever
i am a shorebird enrapt with the migration
roaming you feels an awful lot like coming home

brackish in the cold room
i leach your warmth and feed your flame
the tumble of logs combusts in judders
as the waves come crashing in

it's an arch of a back
and a grasping gasp
i am there at the water's edge
call me singed; colour me burnt

Mary Cresswell

Walk carefully, winter

What we once called
black canyons
cover the road

unseen hotspots
make pitfalls that
surface above them all

dissolving mist
reaching the rocks
three miles below.

Dead souls collect
swell and surge
plunging in freefall.

We, for whom spectra
clatter down too deep
for tracking to evening,

mark another day
waiting for a sunrise
so far invisible.

Cathy

Maybe she was not a monster
solving intricate faults in the
fabric, cut on the bias.

There could be more to her claws
and the silver scratch in her forehead.

After all, it was your saying 'she was a
monster' that actualised our thoughts,
and the way she amputated flowers.

In the garden Cathy was a stake in the earth
and knew things so temporary that stillness
was mastered until the last peep of sunset curled.

As the world slept, she twisted the doorknob
in the violent caving silence 'til it clicked,
and the darkness took a breath and held it.

Our turbid eyes watched, as we've seen it before;
the way moonlight will improvise with a face:
angles stretch their joints and get long on the wall,

a nose and feet compete in the quiet — they lunge
in perfect unison with the gumption of a freak.

Maybe she was not a monster in the way she spoke
with infected actions, like those that carried her off
to new hands and new spires, that broke the morning air.

Jodie Dalgleish

Eben der / The one, and the same

for Joanna Margaret Paul, after her watercolour Eben der

the very one, with
pooling jade curves contouring a teapot
tipping its bird's-head lid towards its sprout of a
handle aerofoiling a foliate distance to a nearby
Iris curving its standard petals down to its perianth's
compound blue light trick as the everyday drop of its
tongue crosshatched on glass as a lepidopteran wing on
the bowl of the vase/jar/mug of a wide cylindrical
container's strokes of colour and graphite lines that extend
to lip light's edges through a translucent 'cup'
sat below the bowl of citrus fruits piled up for one to eat
the parenthetical sweet pea that's mulling over its particular
pigment upflown to its rosy *odoratus* beside an
aquarish-blue echium tipping its bugloss down
to the open throat of a nectareous nasturtium

intricate nasturtium, seen and eaten for its
spurred calyx of a polypetalous corolla, with its nectary,
sucked for its nectar, where there's
the snip of a spur even, *eben*: like I'm trailing the calyx (hold)
of a 'beloved', even, in each object: *der*, that's
the dear 'definite article'; der, die, das, like this is love, love, love.

BIOLUMINESCENCE AT THE BAY

in memory of John Morris

1

Over seventy years ago
the sand was just as wet
fine and compacted
by the outgoing
shallow tide.

2

A colonial style homestead
which may or may not
have been their family bach
is perched just above
the eroding high tide mark.

3

What has gone
and cannot return
is fishing one night
and the line
sliding down deep
into the neon blue sea
illuminated by a myriad
of phosphorescent bubbles —
a magic moment
that caught no fish.

Brecon Dobbie

Chinese Medicine

It's the smell I remember mainly. That remedial
perfume which snuck around corridors and made
your eyes water. It was camphor and methanol, woody
and intense, like eucalyptus. The heat emanating out
from your skin when Mum placed it at the base of your
neck or rubbed it in tiny circles over your temples. *It's
alright, you're alright*, she'd whisper.

Buk Buk wore it
behind her ears, so Mum says. Sitting in her sunken
armchair, her knees bent at a perfect right angle. The
living room is a blur, and the bathroom scared me. We
didn't share a language. Not really. Only the occasional
dor jeh when she'd hand us our lucky red envelopes on
Chinese New Year. She watched over us all at Christmas,
content to be silent in her participation. And it's hard
to imagine her now, retrospectively, all these years later.
Por Por says she was good at knitting. She made jumpers
with no patterns, just the vision in her head. Or how
she'd take one of the chickens from the garden, break
its neck, boil it, pluck it, cook it, then dish it out for dinner
that same night. Unbelievable. That she was once so
alive. When she died, I remember seeing her bed empty. It
was too neat around the corners. At nine, you don't
have a clue. And then, you just move on. But I still think
about her. Those big square glasses, their glossy shine.
How every time we visited, we'd walk over to her in
a line. I'd lean in to kiss her, feel the soft leathery touch
of her cheek against my own. And there it would be, *that
smell*, familiar and concrete. She smiles. She takes
my hand.

fake plastic whale heart

last week at the museum
I tried to climb into the whale heart
and sit inside with my toddler
having one of those moments
where he says something didactic and simple
but profoundly meaningful in a universal way
and I smile knowingly
saying *that's right, kiddo, that's right*
thinking of grown-up problems like bills
or illicit affairs or the crushing, bittersweet weight
of knowing that everything in the fridge and bathroom
belongs to you because you no longer have flatmates
and now that you no longer have flatmates
life is even more expensive
but all he said was *it smells quite stinky in here*
which it did, like armpits of the twelve-and-unders
and before I could even climb in
the museum staff yelled and stopped me
saying it was pretty hard to turn around in there
saying get out, it's just for kids
so he sat alone in the stinky heart
pondering the faded pink plastic
the hazy red light, the shadows
and I sat on the adult allocated black bench
dreaming of my body decomposing into moss
or mushrooms, finally part of a community

people say we all have the same twenty-four hours
but we don't, really
it's like how some babies are named because of religion
and others are named because their parent saw a word
in a washed-out hospital waiting room magazine

and thought it sounded cool without realising it was the title
of a queen with great braids from a popular fantasy
book-turned-tv-show
and before that, a virus deadly to rabbits in the 90s
and what does any of it matter anyway
what will his world look like once I'm gone? will he remember
that summer's day when we sat together
in the swan-shaped paddling pool
when a monarch butterfly landed on his shoulder and
he stayed so still and the water sparkled
and everything felt like a movie?
then he was climbing out, quick as chips
all limbs that grow longer overnight
tousled hair smelling faintly of sweaty plastic
reaching to be picked up
one shoe already missing
and telling me in his tiny voice that sometimes
we have to go in the heart alone
to which I replied
that's right, kiddo, that's right

Ode to the Anti-Vaxxers

During the pandemic
birds in my backyard
conspired against me
flaunting their freedom
while I was in lockdown.

A cloud of blackbirds
rained on my parade
when they stole
my magic beans
and sowed a patch
of oxalis where giants
fear to tread.

A quarrel of sparrows
flung mud from the gutters
shitting on the windows
shitting on the front door
shitting on the welcome mat.

A charm of goldfinches
acted as a subterfuge
for a war party
of pīwakawaka
laying siege
to the strawberries.

A mutation of thrushes
changed their tune
from a romantic
serenade at sunset
to the staccato sound

of an alarm rattle:
I repeat, I repeat, I repeat,
red alert, red alert, red alert,
attack, attack, attack.

O, sweet plovers of paranoia
can these tomtits
of terror be true
or is this bizarre
bird behaviour
just another one
of those garden variety
conspiracy theories.

Death Warmed Up

Party, party, party — and amongst them walking, Mister Death.
Understand: he wants to be your bed companion,
But the door only swings one way for Mister Death.
Beneath the sun, Mister Death's a personality cult of none.
Death might parade naked for your delectation;
Camouflaged in articulation: a grinning skeleton.
Brought up in a moral vacuum, Death never says, never.
Death preens from every mirror; grey panthers patrol the border.

Death, a gambler, stalks and skulks, punter to punter.
Death's nightmare in general is a fear of the funeral.
Yet, no matter how fast, Death comes gaining.
Death's hearse rolls up lickety-split; so, you must hop into it.
Some tussle; some holler; some fight; but all at last lie silent and still.
As, by your hand, Darkness leads you, Death keeps faith with Night.

Amber Esau

Transit

The stars came out
in fuzzy ringlets
blinking raindrops
on an unboned koru
bent towards
the muscly sunset
still dangling
coarse mango slices
that slur & savours
a twisting eel-slick
matchstick evening
while the prayers
old as a row of teeth
chatter the shift
holding themselves
over te moana fou
where the fern
will only briefly
curl

Laura Ferguson

untitled

I need the slip of her skin to find myself
in darkness. Our light hides
to shape new forms, our hallowed tips
reaching to touch. A beckoning groove,
a height to climb and I clamour
so she breathes just like I do.
With scant and fevered motion
to hitch and fall, never ceasing
as we coat our air. Pebbled and inked
we lie entwined, her hands in mine,
gripping silk and iron, knuckles white,
forging pleasure in heat
and I breathe just like her, too.
Featherlight about my shoulders, she is
enlightenment. Found buried,
our divinity flushed in blinding sin.
Potted planter teeth marks score,
harvest bruises waxen from flame.
Splashed searing, mixed media paints as
I watch her eyes widen when I release her soul.
And she breathes just like I do.

Catherine Fitchett

Chlorine

My father's suspended
between wars in a series
of black and white photographs.

He swims up and down,
up and down. Later
he examines each shot with eyes

red-rimmed from chlorine, makes notes
on the back of each one
commenting on details of stroke
and alignment.

My father was too young to remember
the first war. But he sees
returning soldiers, in the streets
and outside the pub,

some missing an arm or a leg, others
wheezing and coughing, their lungs damaged
by gas attacks. The same gas

that keeps the pool water clean. When
the next war comes, there will be new horrors
but my father won't see them.

He reads his Bible, 'thou shalt not kill',
refuses to fight. That war has not come yet.
He swims up and down, up and down

his faith not yet disturbed
by the newsreels — Dachau, Belsen,
Auschwitz — giving himself over to water
which for now is enough to hold him up.

Alexandra Fraser

Lacelost

It's a hibernation of sorts
a flowing of fractals   of thread winding in pattern   without
novelty   tessellating each day
every small pattern-part
the same as the whole

Sleep-making lace   the same gestures
this thread over this
count   count back   again
a Fibonacci thread of diminishing   or increasing
incident   direction doesn't matter

Does the breath-in come before or after the breath-out?

Just breathe

The pattern repeats

Hibernation implies a wakening some-time
wake into spring   into metaphors pushing
up through winter's soil
equinoctial similes branch forth   a flagrant colour-burst

Pattern suffocates each part of speech
they decay from our days leaving skeletal frames

I may not wake
moths will drink my sleeping tears

ASSISTANT

Having been born,
they tuck their hair up under their caps.
Staff have a responsibility for their own health, safety, and wellbeing.

She was born star-like, crayon,
liquid and transparent;
fish swim in her brain, too.

She would've put her cause in with yours,
taking up your cause to the
muting of her own

eyes do dazzle
others who may be affected by her work, research, study and her acts,
omissions,
incidences, near misses, observations,

nonconformities and fires. She flicks a bug off the page, and you
pick your endings,
pick your beginnings.

Her aim was only ever to go away
and to stay
gone.

Michael Giacon

Why cats lead solitary lives

Our conversations, when one-to-one, were under rainbow flags in celebration and talking to each alone in a flushed crowd sipping something white, complex morsels passing on platters perhaps I flirted with the golden rule, divined connection in clever chatter. But now they are itemised one + one = one, their attention for each other, even wary of odd numbers. So it feels when new love is so. Through the debris of the pink parade they swooned, hand-in-hand with happiness. One wore a faux fur headdress of kitten ears while abstracted rainbow wrapped the worked-out chest of + one. They beamed a tandem nod into blinking lights, lorries piled with redundant safety restraints.

Out back in the garden rusted solar lights pulsed crescents of colour on black lawn. Midnight hydrated a dim disquiet. Two silver ovals flashed, a cat picking a damp way to the pond. The yard paused; crickets clicked back on catcalling hush. Crouched on wire netting and mesmerised by bronzed shapes gasping ripples from the murk below, a paw tested barbs circling a space cut for water lilies to rise in brief days of sun worship. Should I stay or go shoo or throw? The cat sat back on its tail and yawned, an urban sphinx over the mystery of mouthfuls and instinct contained, bored with barriers and fun curtailed. Off it pussyfooted to a particular spot and something crunchy in a bountiful bowl to reclaim a place on the warm blanket and purr for chocolate fish floating unnumbered on closed eyes.

Sucking the entire forest into my stupid fucking mouth

I want to tell you all the things I've never
seen before

scratched up from the unknowable
roaming moss beds, lichen thick
and
saying *this is mine*

These bare rocks
shot through with mineral glass
are mine
the black dusk silhouettes
of cliff's crag are mine
in the way
of the
minister's flock
clasped by
expectation
glazed in the clumpy
whiteness
of seabird rocks

I am learning things I know nothing about
and it's confusing

I am learning two waves
pressed against each other
and one must yield

I am learning to be empty
how an absence is invisibly full

I saw colours in the ocean today

I never expected
spindrift flashed through brown and green
the terrifying blue of an arctic melt
Everything is growing
and deteriorating so
rapidly

I scarcely find my footprints
in the crushed sticks and unruly spore

How will anyone know I'm worth
all this trouble?

It is the brilliance of life
that makes us contemplate death

Daring hung over cliff's
crag by a single hand,
kicking
rocks

Oh, it starts out innocently enough
It always does

One day you're filled with the promise
of historical atrocities
next you're idly shifting scrag
into the gullied abyss

There's so much shaping to be done,
I'm unsure whose beginning this is

Living in the gaps left
by ferns and lizards feels
. . . unimportant

I feel suffocated by the possibilities of life
I feel shamed to death by nature

driftwood

i'm worried that one day i'll wake up and realise that
i'm in love with you now until the bitter end.

i can sense it coming
like when all the characters get into a car at the end of a movie
and you've seen enough movies by now to know that
they're going to crash.

i'm worried that one day i'll be left retreading footprints with you
in the sand
each new step expanding the old one just a little
over and over again
until the whole damn beach is just footprint
and there's nothing left for the tide to chase.

i'm worried that one day i'll give up writing bad poems
and wonder if this is what missing you feels like . . .
and if missing you was the cause of it all along . . .

i'm worried that one day i'll watch all that's left of you merely collapse
and be left to wonder what i'm going to do with all my life.

i can feel the worst thing that's ever happened to me getting closer
like a doomed bridal carriage carrying cluster munitions
instead of a bright future together.

i can feel beautiful massacres cropping up at tips of my fingers
i can feel it all falling together again.

one morning after we'd had breakfast — which, like every meal, he ate with his body hunched around the plate in order to protect his food and stake out his territory — Simon told me that I make prison porridge, and so now every weekend as I make porridge I think *prison porridge!*

Simon told me that in prison porridge was made with water and oats and a little bit of salt and served with brown sugar and milk, which is exactly what I do.

he makes his porridge by cooking the oats in a mix of water and milk, which creates a completely different texture to prison porridge, and I can't imagine what that would be like but it seems like some combination of weird and posh.

Simon went to a fancy private school, as well as prison, so it's hard to tell how his water-and-milk porridge recipe came to be.

sometimes I tell other people that I make prison porridge, about how Simon makes it with a mix of water and milk, and every single one screws up their face at his recipe and says *that's just fucking weird.*

I want there to be something in this where Simon heals from the things that pushed him to the murders that put him in prison — which is how we now both know what prison porridge is — or that I heal from Simon and all the ones before Simon and the one after Simon, but this is a poem, not a time machine.

Rebecca Hawkes

That body is booming like business baby

in the land of big mommy milkers and honey
taking advantage of the current interest rates
her bra a dishonesty box padded with crumpled faces
fading queens in pastel menthol spearmint
smushing up to purpled stacks of knighted elder statesmen

they told her she could try on any name
but Venus was already taken
so she tried on some hotter ones Ginger and Pepper
or semiprecious Amber Topaz Ruby Saphyre
settled on Scarlett a letter a readymade woman a ripe mythology

climbing the spotlit pole like a tomato vine on a silver trellis
ripening her bondi sands tan into its most glowing orangey hue
on her sweet navel o her satsuma her clementine
her constituent segments birthed out of clothes discarded like a rind
Aphrodite served ready-salted on the half shell

no longer under her own illusion of glamour
begging dollars from a grubby trackpants pocket
but reeling to rank breath she still leans in
because whomst amongst us hasn't
been repulsed by a key stakeholder

the client the auditor the glorified consultant
alas on nights like this everyone's an external advisor
everyone can identify opportunities for improvement
and tonight her tendered figure is too much
this or not enough that and she should smile more

or her teeth are too bad and she should get them fixed
she should stop smiling so she looks richer
until she can save up to fix them
a gust of beery gingivitis asks her
whether it's very expensive to look that cheap
and then any man she cuts off from the pack

to shepherd into the exorbitant dark backstage
feels like he might be the next to try his hands around her neck
not that there is much leeway for complaint
she has to love her job she has to love herself
and she has to hate her job and has to hate herself

to be respectable and besides if anything really happened
it didn't actually happen to her
and even if it did she earned it
and of course there are those who don't complain
who don't have remembered names

only noted in newsprint for the world's oldest profession
dredged from the silt of the bucolic Avon
their stilled tongues such an affront to decency
those girls girls girls the girls like her
and her sisters whose true names she will never tell

because she doesn't know them herself
as they pass around the strip club's pre-recorded intros
like karaoke microphones or flaming torches
goddess to goddess borrowing each other's archetypes
never staying stuck under one label for too long

playing the old tracks in the long game
shedding their skins in vampire hours
the girls the girls the girls those blacklight angels
wiping her tears without smudging her eyeliner
leading her upwards keeping her back straight

teaching her to walk taller inch by inch
bequesting her their ever-higher heels
rhinestones flaking off the pistol-shaped stilettos
and little ammunition rounds studding the ankle strap
the girls who change their whole nights with their outfits

paint their smiles back on and text their reliable patrons
reeling in the rent from the bad boys the bastards
the broken hearted beaus and boozehound benefactors
lush liquored blood being the ultimate patron of the arts
so those girls can go home richer with the birdsong

lips caked with spittle and glitter and Scarlett
curls up in a mound of wet towels and duvets and
decants the last salty debris from a packet of crisps into her palm
to feed herself from her own open hand as ardent
as the half-wild horse and gentle as the child
reaching a fistful of stolen clover over the electric fence

just before all she knew
when she was thrown back by the shock of it
was that from now on her bones would glow at night

Liam Hinton

death of a salesperson

I

when The World falls apart/ it will fall apart the same way a person does

become destitute/ turn out pockets/ run fingers through unwashed hair/ curl them into fists as they reach the back of the skull/ follicles tugged to breaking point

it will feel the yellow cling of sweat in its pits/ glands clogged and swollen by the heavy metal aerosols/ an oily shaving rash stinging cold/ chemical/ the only dry skin/ a scratch behind The World's knees

bills are mounting/ can't settle the mortgage/ the car/ the air/ expenses that won't be written off/ no liquid capital to coast on 'til next quarter

The World will default/ peep through the blinds for debtors/ day-drunk off brown liquor/ no ice/ left barefoot/ secreting tracks on the hardwood floor/ fuses blown/ tv and radio tuned to a great crunching/ down

II

The World will piss at the air-con/ and unbalanced books/ for their spewing dry heat/ hurl a three-speed desk fan cross the home office/ and leave out the back door/ with plans to spend the bottom dollar on a twenty pack of JPS reds/ and a nip of Jameson/ after it takes some pills it shouldn't have

it will grind the enamel of its teeth/ hard/ up in line at the register/ dig nails into palms/ squeeze knuckles white/ then shake its head/ ask where it is/ despite being a mere three/ maybe four blocks from home people will say sir/ to The World/ as it stumbles out the shopfront/ like a question clinging to the nearest passer-by/ its grubby hands stretching the fabric of a white woman's Chanel blouse/ trying to wipe diesel features from its face/ vomiting oil/ fluoxetine/ adderall/ onto the lenses/ of her Dolce & Gabbana eyes/

The World will babble incoherently in an invented language/ its mouth contorting into dreadful foreign shapes

III

(*this language will create objects in your head/ place a pressure on your neck/ and a granular feeling in the back of your mouth somewhere/ swallowing/ won't wet

there will be some truth to the babble/ some small disquieting truth/ that will keep you in the thresh of a night/ weeks from now/ scouring the pages of a motel bible/ writ in aramaic/ rolling atop the bedsheets as you burn/ both sides of the pillow/ hotter than hell

The World has thrown a breaker/ the arm of a grenade/ Time put beneath your ribs/ now every echoing throb of heart will be quicker than the last/ till there is only a hum held fever pitch

your blood will hump this truth through cholesterol slagged arteries at speed of poison)

you will help this passer-by/ rip The World and its screaming from her/ pinning it to the ground under your weight/ while she calls the police/ shrieking down the line for tasers/ and a social worker/ hoping in secret that somebody brings a gun

(*your shirt button will fall casualty to this schizophrenic wrestle/ one with an image of the sky entombed beneath the plastic/ for a moment you will recall Jacob's back-alley skirmish against the angel/ you worry you will lose your name come dawn)

IV

The World will grapple free and run/ lest it be shot down in the street/ knees skidding across tarmac/ but it will know somewhere deep inside/ its number is up/ that things are closing in

it will climb into its car/ sweep the detritus of fast-food meals from the hood of the dash and slam the accelerator down through a sea of beer cans/ without shifting the stick to reverse

The World may catch a glimpse of itself in the rearview/ lock eyes in such a way that time freezes/ manifests a radiation/ temples whining with the crack of particle decay

The World's skin will melt like wax/ eyes dribbling from their sockets/ the sky outside a fire/ before it slams its car/ full speed/ headlong into brick/ neck snapped ninety degrees/ right-angled with broken glass and nothing

Chris Holdaway

Time crystals and bullshit jobs

A world without science fiction vanishes thus
The most meaningful rules of smoke yield
Dignity in disappearance. Fried social values;
Tabloid debts; contrived particles; perpetual
Motion of resentment — all hell in an accurate
Description . . . .
It stands to reason that crystalline structures
Exist in time as well as space — the fall in
Variance between gainful simulation and being
Driven to a new phase of matter. This the meat
Of economic theory: your waking hours con
-ceived of the same equations governing stars'
Original symmetry . . . .
In this year of the working week does not
The diamond stand for all our doctrines and
Machines? Where clocks fail we have the most
Genuine object: the endless charge of meaning
-lessness that comes with destructive amounts
Of time . . . .
In the ballpark of never: I made up the profit
Motive as a joke that got out of hands in pockets
As if a headline or mathematical proof waiting
Beyond the veil for the right morality tales —
For in administration lies the mystery. Paper
Pushing cosmology; all-night public relations:
Inefficiency the most sacred duty when faced
With the technicality of everyone else. A new
Angle on nature where a reflection has nothing
To do with a clear picture — electromagnetic
Fields forever . . . .
This — all as a battery runs out. We have every
Reason to believe in the abundance of spiritual

Damage; the resurrection of time in the jewel
Of industry burning a whole new category of
Temperature . . . For nothing but equality lies
At the very end of everything.

Alice Hooton

Hills Calm Green

an outgoing tide combs silver
the grey braids of estuary

remember yes
I will always remember

that last Saturday when
from your bed by the window

we watched godwits
a numberless flock

of migrating *godwits* rise
circle fly slowly northward

once summer
filled these rooms with light

now evenings darken

tomorrow
I must leave this place

what will I do
what will I do

with the rest
of my empty life

Part-lament for the girl who dreamt she was a hermit-crab

The dunes at the end of Tovey Street are covered in bunny-tail grass and networks of bright-pink ice plant. The sandy peaks are hard for small legs to climb, each self-made foothold prone to slipping out from underneath you. Here, dad bundles me in a picnic blanket to watch the sunrise over the South New Brighton pier.

I cup this moment in my hands like a small secret fire. It remains despite everything else. I am here and I am still a beachcomber. Rockpools never stopped calling my name.

Six sounds like sex in a kiwi accent

This poem is 6 feet under my high school
It has reserved its spot
Next to the few in my year
Who killed themselves.
It's all tied up in pretty
school pride colours
of black and blood.
This poem is my high school diploma.

This poem is 6 feet under
football studs.
Studs that track over social sport soil.
Studs who track who scores the most.
Studs that see the
loose and ready,
upturned and dirty,
easy to get
6 in deep,
or silver-tongued cleats getting
6 goals in
on light soil skin.

This poem is 6 feet under
the breeding grounds
and the man up motto:
Sapiens fortunam fingit sibi.
Which roughly translates to:
Sink or swim,
and we will take credit for the victors.
But it's in Latin so,
be inspired, I guess.

This poem is 6 feet under
an 'emotional haka' video
with 3 million views.
Look, mate.
Your name is famous.
It's buried under the assembly
where we mourned a kid named 'Jarod'
who was year 12, apparently.
Buried under the best friend and mother
who requested nothing be said.
So they changed your name and year.
So they can show how much they care about you,
'Jarod'.

This poem is 6 feet under
the curious thought of why no one else
would want to be a girl.
Just to see what it's like.
Just to be delicate.
Just to know how the studs feel
on soft soil skin.
But this poem isn't educated enough
to tell you why.

This poem is a eulogy written
in the fine print of your enrolment.
This poem is etched into your tombstone
in the early graveyard plot.
This poem is the worst years of your life
that you wish you could relive.
This poem is casually homophobic for a laugh,
This poem works out and fucks,

This poem knows how to throw a punch,
This poem has vodka in its drink bottle,
This poem has a rape allegation.
This poem cannot be unlearnt or
RetrievedRetriedRecalledRelocatedRepeatedRevived,
This poem is buried
6 feet under tear ducts.

This poem is coming out
in an open casket.

About growing up, son

The small chamber I made you is nearly empty.
The shreds of you are tucked in
the pores of our walls. It smells of you
and it holds your shape. You are not old
enough to know you can come back.
You must take everything and run
on your chicken legs. Only when
you notice your feet — how strong! how splayed! —
will you be ready to return, rolling
your shoulders, your flapping shirt leaving
etchings of feathery strips and
extraordinary patterns on the walls.

Lincoln Jaques

Advertisement for Bus Driving

My brother the bus driver
calls me on his break
he's sitting somewhere out there
in the canyon of an empty city
at a bus stop under a billboard
advertising for more bus drivers.

A twelve-hour shift and the knee's
like a bastard, he complains. It's
all the pushing on the accelerator.
For 30 years he's driven
over the harbour bridge, back
and forth like Sisyphus and his rock.

The drivers he's worked with have been
knifed, spat at, sworn at, called all the creative
racist slurs under the sun. Some have been beaten
to death. Tonight, he says, someone pissed in his doorway.
A couple fucked on the back seat. Addicts
shared needles in the mobility impaired seats.
A drunk chundered in the aisle, smiled as he rolled
off at Vic Park to crash under the trees.

Who'd want this job? he says. He's said that for 30 years.
My brother needs a knee replacement. His eyes are shot.
Cataracts; retina detachments. They keep him on.
The doctors sign off his certificates. They get paid.
Someone's got to shunt the masses. During lockdowns
they closed all the public loos. The drivers had to hold
on for 12-hour shifts. Buses everywhere idling next
to parks or alleyways, the drivers getting shanked
while urinating against tombstones. In lockdowns
they'd drive that 12-hour shift alone.

That was good, says my bro. *But too much time to think.*
I thought about my life, all the bad shit. All alone out here.
It does things to you. I thought of Sisyphus again.
How he cheated death by chaining it up. How the Gods
punished Sisyphus by setting him to roll his stone.
Maybe my brother's punishment for cheating death
for 30 years of driving buses is to keep driving them
back and forth across the bridge for 12-hour shifts.

Often I imagine my brother still out there,
driving through the night,
long after we're all gone.

Claudia Jardine

Puttanesca

I have come to this flat where some of your friends are hanging out to sit and let the good wine I drank at the Department's Christmas Party burn off me. One guest reports that he is 'sick of how shocked everyone acts about stuff', and his example is the Holocaust. While he is in his hole, he complains piteously about the tendency of others to be 'triggered' by such discussions. Your shirt buttons are set to summer, your Star of David hangs flat between your collarbones. Neither of us know why this man is here, but you feed him anyway. Our host tries to balance his plate on the arm of the sofa. The plate tips and a large portion of puttanesca slides straight into his lap. Our host is so drunk, he cannot be shocked. His girlfriend scoops up the food with her hands and slaps it back on the plate. No one worries about the stains. It is not that sort of place. You are offering to walk me home. As we move I watch for auspices. Two snails climb a wall. Some wingshape passes overhead. A stranger approaches with a bleeding leg. You leave me at my door. Each step, hallway and window frame feels like a tiny bereavement.

Amanda Joshua

In search of home

Like to walk down this road in Mt Eden
Sprawling villas, small brick-laden
paths trailing to wrap around porches
There's a woman perched on that one
Messy-haired and laughing
by her squirming 3-year-old
Follow Kendrick Lamar blasting
2 homes down
To a lanky, beanie-headed boy
spraying the left side of his garage
a furious purple
Lavender lines the windows
of this cottage
And there are books lining
softly pink walls
Stretch on tiptoes
for a glimpse of who could be
Stacking Dr Phil by Jane Austen
Not judging they're both
great for self-help
All this life tucked away
inside even
that awkward apartment complex
Wonder who has dominion
over the blowing laundry
on their shared clothesline
Pause 1 house over for
heart work gone into
carefully weeded flowerbeds
where marigolds doze
Who chose the colours

on that stained glass door?
Move on before the steaming mug's drinker
can return to their home office
The girl by her lemon tree
teaching herself guitar the work
it takes to learn to build a life
It makes me so hungry that
I linger by a house with its porch light on
The cars all safely home
So much warmth in the voices
bleeding from the living room
Force myself to walk on
before they can begin to wonder if
I'm casing the joint

december 20th

carl sagan — you died the day i was born
well, exactly a year before it.

i wish i were you reincarnated
but all i love is poetry
and space as, like, a metaphor —
the real thing
too mathematical.

i just try to open and write
surrounded by all! those! stars!
there are more of them
than sand grains,
you once said.

i wish you could see
the new, jww images with your kind eyes
space is now hi-res resplendent,
how you would have loved it.

carl, i have often wanted
to be free floating in cosmic soup
like dave in *2001*
or you, since 1996.
touching everything; holding nothing.

but somehow
cosmos made me feel
the right amount of large/small, and i thought
may as well do something
with this precious gift, consciousness.

so i went and saw the stars
the best i can from here —
in freezing tekapo i was confused
on a hill in a red rented snowsuit
waiting to feel the universe.

carl, i know you're not up there above
you don't watch or care
as your atoms bounce around,
maybe brushing into
a person or two.

anyway, carl, today is my birthday again.
so i'm another year older, and you —
you're another year gone.

Ōākura Beach

That space asks for something to enter it.
I imagine people walking with clean washing
towards the sea.

Sheets are coloured by the sky's reflection.
Children dragging sticks behind them,
faced with distance,
sever wind-blown lips.

This is the first day of my lonely spell.
Seagulls are locked above like cut-outs.

There is nobody around really. Extinction
is the only thing on the beach.

The wind tucks its fingers into the space
between an ocean and a home.
I see it slide through the people I've imagined.
It whispers an imperative.

Robert Kempen

Nimbuses

Once kept hanging
over everything Auckland
    down-pouring the rains

a one day that wasn't
on & on into six
    in irregular intervals

pools in their apparent
in the unwanted
    here & there

as if these were wanting
to lay waste anything material
    disparate to Eliot's 'The Waste Land'

surely not the same
with his statement
    'is of rhythmical rumbling'

floating carry-ons,
reminiscent Constable's cumuli
    in the vast receding landscapes

whilst the everything city in a time
just incomparable to Venice's —
something was making
    the most of it

in their here & there
upping & fresh smelling
  sprightly & brightly,
  brilliant green blades

the non-smoking & anti-law —

Pet Theories

A 'pet theory' isn't a speculation one repeatedly returns to;
it's a theory about the meaning of pethood. I have been a pet
for many years now, in the sense that I am not responsible
enough to care for myself. I wasn't brought up badly, but I probably
spent too much time following desirable sunbeams around
the front room and swatting myself in the mirror, and not enough time
getting scout badges for fire-lighting or doing explosive ordnance
disposal courses during the summers, or whatever everyone else
does to manage having been born and being expected to continue
to live. Much of life is a great strain on my nerves unless I sleep
in a little basket on the floor for sixteen hours a day — I don't mind
confessing that. This has informed my thinking on pethood.
It's sad that we only take a genuine interest in things when they
affect us personally, like a friend who gets a free kickboxing lesson
and now wants to kickbox you all the time, but that's how it is.
So what it means to be a pet is big for me, a real brain-crowding
superissue that has required many agonising rounds of deliberation.
I have sweated. I have wrung my hands. I have burned 90%
of my calories thinking about it, and the remaining 10% writing down
the thinking. I can offer a statement of clemency and wonderment:
you don't need a glossy coat or exquisite plumage to be a pet.
Just a look that says *I will reward protection with a warmth
that is hard to understand.*

nana's kai

I look for you in the sky
drawing you with shooting stars
knead like my cat at midnight
seeking
your galactic colostrum
to supplement patinaed scenes
of us alone
with afterschool caramel popcorn
curving on your hose spray lawn
you lifted my crop top
unconvinced
rolled your eyes like a rainbow
elastic recoils
slapping shut my bluey camel mole
obscene pink meat
The kuratahi street plum tree you fed us
liquid under its hedonistic shade
mokopuna spit pips like bird shit
for you to step on hanging the line
ogled your damp t-shirt sized knickers
that veil the celestial slide
where our mothers came out
can you know those 8-year-old
fat pudding tits
bore sparse black hairs
not plums
Spooned me kawa rhubarb on formica
screwed up cheeks tempered with ice-cream
quiet vanilla
festers
a glacial creep
blanching outside in
long-gone nana

this frizzy polynesian tendril
psychic diaspora in her heirloom maara
placenta clotted fingers
sinks in the clay
Caked heels ascend the sagging porch
earthen debris left in wake
I retrace the passages in your empty whare
calling
no sound but
ancient fridge
electric
dial tone.

the long-term implications of this forecast are not yet known

I wish you weren't going to show me your way of feeling love. with its low over a strong ridge of high to poor visibility. the lights could be dimmed for a while. perhaps it turns out it wasn't my long sightedness over the swell rising but rather your listening. would you not hear me if I was to say you don't need more sugar, honey. surprisingly you may say, I am astounded at the cheapness of such beverages. I predict the sea will instantly become rough. I wish you were never going to show me your way of feeling with its history of broken yellow lines, that could at any moment change to a gale, without such thing as a warning enforced. if the outlook was to rise and you said that I am lovely, it would not be the same as I love you. you see, one day easing, another day fair visibility, clear east-west, followed by south-west followed by moderate at times, followed by a misleading calm, then suddenly becoming rough again. I really do wish you weren't going to show me your style of love, this drawing me in over a surface that's everywhere developing. your current outlook being twenty-five knots rough, on repeat. and that telling of sins you do as the revealing of secrets early on does not mean you're one to trust. it is rather more likely a potential gauge, that may well lead to periods of rain. it's 35 knots in my belly and your outlook is all patchy rain and drizzle. take me back and I would follow my word with my body. I would not be persuaded to strip naked in such climate preferring instead to float for a while, easing for a time until say, separation point.

5 o'clock at Iwami Ginzan

A low voice in the tunnel, a chuckle
responds. Both ticket-sellers are checking

for stragglers, to shepherd them back to
the wet heat I jogged through again

to reach this shut gate in the mountain.
The veins of silver, the map board explains

are exhausted. Through the gate's iron lattice:
the small talk, and this breeze wringing

my body of the slope that began beside
a temple. That one packed with

squat statues of miners. They are still
tickled by spots that crawled round their insides.

Five hundred and one stone mouths.
Many chiselled into smiles.

Elizabeth Kirkby-McLeod

Ancestors

Anyone but Anne Carson do poetry?
Epigraphs, quoted stances
cited favourites
another
another
another
I refuse to buy
another
book that calls forth this Canadian!

It's not Anne's fault, she seems delightful
but why are you ashamed
of our ancestors, who trod the same streets as us
exited the same small towns? I sit with a puzzled
expert: *we don't see this in our other*
territories, they devour their writers.

You travel to Paris to lay fresh flowers
on Wilde's tame tomb, layover in London to tour
Keats' house. Meanwhile, in Aotearoa
history is dissolving in each fresh southerly.

A tiny resistance leader
I stand in a playground and say: *look at this tree*
planted for Elsie, remember her book?
I make us stop at every forgotten plaque.

And who was that woman passing us
on her way to the swings? It's our very own
Anne! Who last raised her flag to signal their
whakapapa?

They cannot navigate
by our stars, those northerners
why
why
why
still long to sail
under their breeze?

Casting

I thought I was that character in a Hallmark movie. You know, the one who moves back to her hometown from the city, after her troubled marriage breaks up, to heal and raise her precocious children. The one who has been good, and although sad, still smiles at her family's antics while making a cooked breakfast before work. There was meant to be a local handyman who worked for my parents, or a powerful boss with a hardened heart to tousle the kids' hair and fix my sink. I would bump into him at holiday events and he would play the guitar on my porch.

But the script wasn't delivered, or wasn't learned. They don't know that they have to look fondly at the children. Or to watch me making dinner in jeans, flour on my check, with a look of longing. No one told them that you kiss in a band rotunda, not grope in the bathroom. That you stay up all night talking instead of fucking. That stubbornness and independence are stock character traits to be admired. That if they break through the walls of my hurt heart, there will be softness and swelling music.

So, maybe I'm the supporting character. The eccentric neighbour who shows up unannounced with a bottle of wine. The work friend who gives advice and is often seen in split screen on the other end of a phone. The sister to meet for coffee. The soccer mum to chat with at games. The best friend who ends up with the leading man's best friend, even though he is a little bit tubby and bald. The one who fades into soft focus, as the C
grade celebrities drive off
into the sunset.

When stars no longer

In his later years,
my uncle the war historian, could often be found
on a hot summer's day, in his upstairs study
where he stepped back from his desk,
    from starvation and massacre, genocide —
    vast battles, last century's slaughter
and with one eye to the eyepiece of his telescope
aimed, not at the sky, but at the curve of beach
below the house, where he imagined himself
close to the cool waves, barefoot in white sand,
and joyous amidst an array of flesh-clad beauty

With an eye fixed, he went back beyond the years
    beyond Churchill and Eisenhower,
    political wranglings and propaganda
to where his mother no longer accompanied him
with her tartan rug and her club sandwiches, scones
and a thermos of hot tea. Where he was at last so close
he could see the dimple form on her cheek, as though
he had just walked up to her. The tug of tight cotton
across her breasts. The way she ran in slow motion
over the sand without any intent to escape. And
the way she moved, in and out of his view, such that
he would lift the tripod in his arms, and together
they would dance around the room.

Wes Lee

A Naked Wish

The wind-chimes from *Body Heat.*
A disembodied voice behind the curtain at A&E
crying: *Am I going to die?*
Lucian Freud on his deathbed. They took the paintbrush from
his hand. He kept trying to get back to his studio to paint.
I was happiest when I was ill — with you, playing your guitar
beside the bed.
At the start of the song I am already thinking about when it ends.
I conjure Meryl Streep in *August: Osage County*
flailing across the flat prairie,
Julia Roberts looking on from the car.
The horse this morning, clattering, rearing up, whipping
fear into the road.
I wanted to shout at the rider but kept my mouth shut for fear
she would think me
mad — or old.
To live now is to live in disguise.
It is difficult to hold on to the wild in the body.
That sweet death smell at the gate. Freesias have that sweet
death smell.
Death or shit?
Heart,
you control each breath of my life.
The interminable shunt of the production line, the jiggle
of bottles.
A jukebox unplugged from the whirligig, dancing
to the same song, spinning alone.
The island purple and harsh, cut from the sky.
It was my mother I was afraid of.
I count the hours I've slept
on my fingers.
The days number, the days compress.

We are greedy for days.
I dreamed of being old. The inside of a car —
you and I.
Strange how perfume should appear in the air,
putting things down here, writing of you.
A naked wish, as if you are standing
before the light of the birthday cake or have the wishbone
crooked.

Blank parchment

Rage, rage against the dying of the light.
— Dylan Thomas

There is nothing outrageous about death:
simply a return
to what we always were
on borrowed time.

The picture you drew of us
you and your granddad
now covers a gap
on the fridge door.

I love you too.

I love the time
you took out
to fashion the expanse
of a sheet of white paper.

Outside it takes little
effort to tear away scraps
of the pale, ridged skin
of a paper birch.

Enough space for a haiku.

The underside is
creamy brown enough
to highlight the fleet black
lettering of any poem.

In these small measures
        of blank parchment
                we write outselves into
the texture of earth.

Easy

ease me into grace, sweet and easy,
lean cut, on the bone, ease me into
release from noise, easy quiet, restful not-noise,
crickets and news-from-the-next-room,
Norwegian dubbed over, easily pointing to the next clue,
so many steps to being easy, good thing
I dug that grave a little while ago, easy to
see what's kept you there for so long, easy, like
a spa bath or asking someone for money,
easy to be tenderly holding your wrist between my teeth
easy, isn't it, to stop being easy to be with, easy
to slip out of or into, out of being easy,
easy was for all comers now I am difficult, easy to love and easier
not to, I listen to children scream from up on the hill
and I ease myself into a new room, easy to live away from her,
difficult to live away from you, eased into putting spikes out,
eased into being thorny, pleased to meet you with my weaponry bristling,
I lie there filled with grace and poise, the soil slowly spilling,
it's not easy to dig for so long, or to ease a body down,
I don't dream of release any more, just to ease my claws into someone
the noise seeps into all the rooms in this house, please
someone add some insulation,
please someone do something
to make things easier for me.

Three card monte

*

I can't remember what I was thinking about
when I lost my virginity on the landing of a staircase. Hard
stone steps, the soft tapestry against which we pressed, importunate.

**

White shirts laundered away from London smoke. The secret of me
is not my clothes. Or even how you know my body through them — a
glancing thought. Branched candlelight.
I talk about you in the first person.

***

In Calais in the first-floor salon the yellowing curtain half-caught by
wind and I by a sudden moment of terrible clarity. The gentlemen
polite, appalled; the house rented. This was towards the end of my
life.

We Levered Pine Needles

The year they untucked
a lump from Mum's throat
        a cat with thumbs
        crept out from the hydrangeas in the garden

She laughed because
she'd never seen a prettier rat
with bigger paws

That spring
we levered pine needles
from the deck slats with our fingernails
Mum collected gravel from the path into her knees

coaxed the cat out with coleslaw containers
of cold milk

So Dad bought a pet bowl on the sly
and Mum wore a blue gown into theatre

helped the doctor
tell her it had been the bad kind of a growth

She came back with a silver thread which hung out
both ends of her neck
lay still and let the cups of tea collect fur islands

        watched the cat blow in and teeter on the pillows

We'll call him Nimbus, she told us
he's a nervous cloud
that might thunder any second

If doors swung shut he bolted
there was a brick to keep the bedroom open to the verandah
        till some visitors walked in and saw stiff hankies on the floor

They brought us buckets of pumpkin soup
which grew skin in the microwave
but that we shovelled into mugs

held on our laps as
duvet picnics swallowed the afternoons

Mum listened with her eyes closed
played Lake Wobegon over the radio
        Nimbus put his head into the cup
        left beside her on the bed
        dyed his eyebrows orange

        curled his paws
        scooped soup

        tremored purrs

So, that's what you're good for
she laughed and

        we laughed
and she held her neck together
with two fingers on her pulse

Finn McWhirter

Threshold

taking off / lions in the engine roaring
the girl next to me / clutches my hand
ribbons in her hair / the colour of secrets

i put 'oblivion — midnight' by alaska reid on repeat

when i can / i always fly at night
night up here / gathers like a garment / and
i begin to feel / so hollow / a good kind of hollow
one that / if someone dropped a stone inside of me
i would be almost certain / you'd hear its echo

my friends lit a candle for me when i left
i wonder if it's still burning

reflection outside of inside / past it
land slowly reducing to a point / everything
is shrouded in silence / because all the strings
that could be singing out / have snapped / to let the moon
sing her silent song

i try not to let anyone see me cry
please don't notice / this silken tear

i can see the seams / holding everything together / i like to
run my fingers over them / to feel the two natures
perilous to one side / visceral to the other / and
the wall between them / beginning to melt

last night i put my dream in a cradle / and
the mobile above it was made of origami cranes

the girl beside me / still hasn't said a word / but
i think she likes / my blue cufflinks / and how they match my tie
she is still holding my hand / while our plane draws this cloud out
slowly pulling it apart / we are here / we are at the threshold

Terra Nullius

There's an island in the gulf,
I'm going there when this is over,
I won't plant any bean rows,
But there'll be pipi and pāua,
Shade along the shoreline.

Why didn't you help me?
I asked you once.

Belong, belong,
The frogs are always asking to belong,
Even at midday,
When no one listens to them anyway.
But the hills have no trees there,
Sheep and colonials, you see,
So I'll plant poplars and willows,
Jasmine and honeysuckle,
The things no one wants anymore,
The things that don't belong.
Or trap the rats,
Watch the bellbirds come back,
Or do nothing and accept,
That on an island of discarded things,
Like the terra nullius of my body,
You thought there was no one there,
But you were wrong.

Khadro Mohamed

Liars

//
intro.

She was born in the humid spring of the late 90s
North of a border
West of a sea bed
East of the setting sun
South of the crescent moon
It happened quickly, faster than the blink of an eye
Her mother's eyes twinkled a little as she gazed down
The tiny pink jelly bean in her hand louder than the birds above
And the curves of her father's lips deepen a little
And the sound of the Arabic Qu'raan fills the air briefly
She cries at her birth, curious eyes watching as her lungs fill with air
for the first time
Her grandmother bottles the sound, runs across the poppy fields
And buries it deep in the earth
Like a seedling
And when she grows strong enough to open her eyes
They see nothing but the warmth of the sunshine and the crisp
breeze of August

1.

It's winter
Mid-July
But I awoke this morning with blooming
palms and fruit trees bursting from
the grooves of my spine.

2.

I watch the horizon from the bay — waiting for snow to cover the Wellington streets again.
It's like I'm waiting for nostalgia to wring me dry
It's like I'm waiting for a storm to rip apart this tiny space of sky and drown me whole.
It's like I'm waiting for the sand to whisper something back to me.
It's like I'm waiting for everything broken to become less broken.
It's like I'm waiting for something to wake me from this sleep

But nothing happens, it's all another broken promise.

3.

There's a print of turmeric in the centre of my palm, crawling slowly up my arm, spreading all of its yellow insides on the curves of my shoulder and down the centre of my back. My mother told me turmeric heals ruptured skin and forgotten tongues — Another lie.

4.

Why is it that every time I look in the mirror I don't see myself:
I see all of the Indian Ocean,   twisted cardamon,   clementine smiles,
          I see goat milk   twisted zulu,   brown sugar skin,
coffee forests   a shade made of banana leaves   I see a continent
       & broken canoes
       Aster skies   white sand   paprika stained fingers
                                   polluted sunsets   & a pollen-soaked breeze

5.

But still, I see nothing of my past self
But still, I'm alone
But still, insomnia drinks me

Your Stars for April

after Cindy Sherman's Untitled Film Still #53

You can find yourself in the wrong place unexpectedly, your coat thrown across a bed and no easy way to leave. You can fix a slight smile on your face and remain quite still while a run works its way up your leg from the hole where your foot turned as you started, mouth a little dry, up the steps to the front door. If you were going to start again, it would not be in this white nylon pin-tucked blouse or following an afternoon reading magazines in your underwear with big rollers in your hair which you had to spray into place with Aqua Net before pulling on a girdle and the skirt that is a little too tight. You'd wear a slinky low-cut dress, and you'd go straight up to him the minute you walked into the room. You wouldn't be watching from the couch under the pretty lamp, legs crossed slant, nursing a tumbler of warm Bacardi and coke. Not smoking, not talking, not looking for trouble.

Josiah Morgan

An excerpt from *Our Year of New Zealand Letters*

I am writing a poem to get better
at separating the unfettered choreography
of electrical signals and their corresponding conditioned-reactive
responses.

Every day there is a list to be ticked slash crossed off
slash kissed on slash kicked off of slash pissed off by. The startling
wave
of these listed splinters tossing up sharp horrors
was not something I ever thought I would know
to destroy, let alone how to.

I am going back to that place
of destruction. I am going back in my poem
to those better years of unchoreographed fettering
in my mother's bedroom in my father's house
listening to Arcade Fire's 'Windowsill' and
I don't want to live in my father's house no more

and I don't want to live
in a world where my poems can't group themselves according to my
need
instead of the needs of others, I don't want to live without
the choreography of getting better being undermined
by the very existence of unchoreographed better days.

I don't want better days
without the promise of some kind of change.
I wake up every day to you leaving
the splintered sun behind you as the door clicks

shut, kettle boiled and tea safely keep-cupped away
but still there remains my coffee to be made, I'll boil afresh

for that. If I'm clever, that might kill the seething
seconds spent worrying this/that/me/list/you, what a fix

that would be, to parse the worry in days
spent like all the others. To start again the mesh

of this poem we've been making together without that heaving
child in my belly riddling worry like that fictive Sphinx

across my teeth, my tongue, your brow. What a display
of love that would be, for me to deny this feeling like that stench

that hangs over the city you leave into. What a way to go
with the rising sun clicking splintered into place and a new day
behind you.

Emma Neale

The Barnum Effect

On a deserted early London morning,
the footpaths ice-rink glossy with dawn rain,
an older man called to me from under shop awnings.

He sashayed, swept off his hat, clasped it to his chest;
'An angel with a broken wing,' he sang.
All I gave was a grin, a quick duck of the head,

the shape of my back from the fast clip
that women are taught says self-possession,
wary, through experience, of men too smooth or flip

and of my own pulse's helter-skelter,
swooping heedlessly
to a crooner's synthetic nectar.

Yet in a particular terracotta autumn light
that ten-second suitor-stranger
still sometimes comes to mind

his tone as if he knew me as soon as he saw me —
although if he understood precisely
how to make-swoon with the song of *anybody*

I think he also sang mostly,
if slantwise,
of himself.

Ellis Ophele

BODY HORROR, THE TRANSFORMATION, THE ABERRANT SEX

The playboy-esque mask I wear to show off my tits. I mean, it's not like I'm attached to them.

You're paying for my surgery.

You're paying for the Poptarts I live on.

The mask I put on so that I can take it off; the relief of finishing.

You're a bombshell man.

You're the type I'd flinch from.

Anyway, I'd rather have a choice, you know? I've seen the way they leer. At least I get to pick what I wear this way. I get to choose the timing.

You're a hawk, I'm the roadkill.

You're a hawthorn bush, I'm the mouth.

Men say I've got that mouth made for holding them inside of, made to be a vehicle of hunger, a phthisis suffered on them. Look at it. Look how delicate. Won't you fund my neuroses, my bad habits? I can't hold a job but I can look good. I can be whatever they want. I'm flexible. Gold instead of antimony. Gold, an ounce beaten into a square metre sheet, thin enough to see through. I'm not a person, I'm not even a ghost, but the hollow building the mask takes grasp of severely.

You're a rifle.

You're the bullet I put between my bared teeth   when I turn on the camera

I'm a rabbit.

Claire Orchard

Floral wallpaper

Doorways let light, people, and weather
in and out, but it's the efforts of a pair
of silver candlesticks, along with
the statement of that occasional chair,
that truly make the room. That

and the twinned, gilt-surround mirrors,
set up in opposition, reflecting everything
to eternity. We made our decisions
about the décor, but in the end
any home boils down to one of two options:
the place you're on your way back to
or the place you're leaving.
All these years of living in the yellow glare
of those entwined fake dahlias and now
here we are, stripping it back

over coffee, the French press diplomatically
tabled midway between us, doing our best
to leave the children out of this, those children
who were never anyway really ours,
who aren't even real children anymore.

A. L. Ping

Penknife

When Grandfather was a young man,
they gave him a little ivory-handled knife.

With this, he cut off the remaining flesh
on his father's exhumed skeleton.

For this homage, they said, our ancestor spirits
will grant propitious fortune.

But inside the urn of cleaned bones,
Grandfather buried his faith in the old ways.

I have been cleaning the bones of my father —
hanging them up high as wind-chimes.

But my father is not yet dead,
and some of the bones, I realise now,

are my own.

Michele Powles

There you are, dancing

for Serie Barford

In a night where the air is thick with women
their eyes daring the world to stop them
tongues lashing the doors
and ceilings
that stood/stand in their way,

there you are.

In a year that surely would have broken
anyone, seen an old scourge take everything/everyone
for its jealous self, eating
soft fried hearts, juicy and tender as chicken thighs
and licking its fingers, fat and deadly-full of your blood,

there you are.

In a life that shines: the moon, a star,
you speak of the thin edge of existence,
of the work
that is to be done
to bring te rongoā and ivory walled hospital views together

your skin is a luminous casing, letting
clear light shimmer onto ripe bruises
and demanding we look,
look at what has brought us here

instead of letting old curses
bare down,
heavy and loud
you grow bigger,

you have become giant.

There you are,
with your newly wired hair
holding time captive until
you have finished the work.

There you are,
in your grace and bare feet
gulping mouthful after mouthful of
the promise of death
to show how it can/might/would be
done.

There you are,
dancing
on the sharp ridge
between above
and below.

Beautiful, urgent, fierce hope,
there you are.

put that in your pipe & smoke it

not me, but smoke from the wet woods, resinous scraps, flakes in the black wind.
i scratched the matchbox, sucked the sulphur. i don't belong in this picture

pressed to the glass, so close you don't notice. it might be carpet burn
hooked fingers. the inner vision that cracks the egg
that shakes the nest from its tree.

the child that stones the hive.
i carry a knife to skin the persimmon with, the crisp apple red with liquid vitamin.
cut loose skeins of bush weed, streams that circumnavigate the city.

from the top floor i'm high enough to touch everything.
all of it. drop, caught by the flagstones. remain anonymous.

relive the experience in a parachute.
rise like tuff grass sprung in its cracked electrics
signals that covet the memory.

i *am* the resurrection. tortured, irritable at the station. signing some papers:
you must not deny the body

America Doesn't Love You

I wonder if Lana Del Rey knows about it;
here we have a girl who was a baby once,
how unique she is in that prospect.

A young thing,
who has pretty things
overturned

uppity, she is
with her long hair and fingernails,
watching lanyards and flagg-
ed posts
pass by her window she is

tensing cheeks and her stomach
sleeping and grinding teeth,
breathing in carcinogens
from Dad's barbecue.

and I don't compete like they want me to
I try alternative forms of control
I prefer to flex certain muscles of mine.

Me and her we're tight you see,
and we want the same things:
five dollar rings that turn our fingers green,
chocolate cake (and blood and guts)
the right to devour
all the on-demand sushi roe
and wade into seafoam.

Seafoam can be red
and red and white and blue
are familiar colours
in some flags
(just thought I'd remind you.)

I've been laughing and waiting for later

It's almost disappointing when the storm
doesn't come, my umbrella all set
to become an épée cutting the rain
to filaments, the sky metallic and armed
then nothing, a teacher not arriving
to teach and the class amok, it's chaos.

Walking in circles in a cornfield was
the last time I knew I'd cried, the brown
champagne husks spilling into the rows
and I was so thoroughly lost, I felt the
gathering wetness in my mouth and eyes
and there was no one there to stop me.

Leaning against a cold concrete fence
with my wife leaving me inside, I must have
when a boy I owed died in his kitchen
but these feel more like promises than
memories, seeing a train I should be on
leaving while I am still on the stairs.

Erin Ramsay

The Green Land

the apple slices cut and the plastic straws,
coloured and made white by bending and the
wide bowl of Onepoto Basin with a slide ten
storeys high in the middle. But they lied to us
because the world doesn't end at St. Heliers
or the easy suburbs of Mount Eden with no
street-names or even Whangārei in the
summer. The tracks on *Nature's Best* from
the eighties weren't made by neat men who
had it all figured out but by kids living in shit
flats in Dunedin wearing corduroy. There is
no place for the shy only networking in
offices and house parties and the death knell
of cataclysmic world events is a parasitic fist
banging on your window. They ripped up the
tramlines in 1956 and should you have a kid.
Buying wooden toys for her when she is five
if someone will love me through my tears
and I might have a beard by then and the soft
eyes of a father but I don't want to carry it
myself. Here is Mario Alejandro Ariza
saying that Miami is falling to the sea's
suffocation and the manholes lift into the sky
with violence when it is raining and if I took
a hammer and smashed all the polypropylene
toys I sold at Whitcoulls when I was a
teenager they would laugh at me in pieces
and hide in my own flesh and blood. Silicon
Valley is a liar who doesn't pay his taxes and
it was Te Kopua-o-Matakerepo not The
Basin all along but the old Pākehā covered
their eyes and called in to talk-back radio to
complain. It was tino rangatiratanga all along

but the YouTube algorithm told them gravity
wasn't real and they swung paving stones in
arcs towards Parliament. Anger is unoriginal
and everyone has lost grandmothers before
you and you are the strongest person you
have ever known, refusing the grey sky's call
to suicide. And the unoriginal is plentiful like
the feelings of joy hearing kākā and one
hopped closer on the deck, I can walk up the
steps without fear. There is the green land,
forward in the palimpsest of time around
Pōneke's jaw of the ray. All your frustration,
the dry organisation of social change and the
emails you sent rising invisible to burn the
heads of the hydra and beat back Manchin,
the oligarchs and amorality. The films
watched with flatmates, their promises to
look out for you and here I see you reading
on your favourite autumn morning the tale of
the lighthouse again. Video calling your
parents for as long as you need to. Bodies
that matter, fuck networking and the char of
irony and now there are the conversations
where you felt something safe and beautiful,
the ring of faces. *Normal is a fiction*, here he
brings chocolates all the way from Rome.
One day you will fail to tell the truth in your
imagined land, placing sandwiches in pouaka
kai for your younger equal. Food without
judgement you hope and their favourite
things, maybe lemon cake and to the left
there will be

@hine: They never were don3 up like that

after Cassandra Barnett's 'space rake'

hinemo or hin3mo4n4
what texted nightmare what farflung star
have ia pulled or pull in2 ia ocean
ia want to undone pulled apart by taangata
ia wants to be or bee or made in2 the past tense
iaia creates large gaps between ia and ia exes
make tukutuku (lol) panel out of
the memories of ia
bodies
hinemo takes all ia love and places it in a box ia is saving
from/for the world
the world
the world
the wor d

ia mokopuna a secret in the back of f ram e
does hinemo have access to the dark waters

the ferryman rivers o river drift ia a l o n g time coming un
done would ia sunbake a tattoo
into ia shoulder while waiting to sea/see/c++
a tangatatangatababbler ia remembers
th touch of
curious pop
o curious pop up in ia mind
th roro/hine/ngaro
iarere pull down star and make glow in under

ia wishes to swallow tangatatangatababbler whole would that make
ia complete again ia is not sure the babblertangata ia loved with
ia whole heart unzipped like winrar and ia extracted all ia could

before like th river   like th awa moving on
dragging th ocean behind
                    ia lovedrag
                    ia pulls on ate tau
                    ia will not be pinned to this
                    iaiaiaiaiaiaiaiaiaiaiaia

Vaughan Rapatahana

bury me

bury me in Pātea,
near where my placenta was   biffed
                                        into some sack
& incinerated in the furnace.
inter me at the annex
that is no longer there.

bury me at Tutua,
somewhere by the urupā.
inhume me under the ancient pōhutukawa
                                                        l i n g e r i n g
near that *fluctuant* fenceline
we painted all those years ago.

bury me close by Tin Yan
upon that hill of concrete mausoleums.
glimpsing the night lights
                                        of Shenzhen,
when they're not g r a p e s h o t
by the gloom.

bury me in J. Pineda
out back among the papaya trees
weeping themselves   silly
                over the pos tpo ne d stone wall
that lopes around the house.

bury me   anywhere
that is not some anaemic cemetery
ruled in straight lines
by white men in black suits,
with dog collars

chained to religious sanctimony.
glossators
who feign their every single word
about the dead,

rise
who might just ^ again
& avenge
their immiseration.

Words of consolation

you are wheelchaired
steel coracle locked
Up the creek without a paddle tra la
in your 4 by 6
penitentiary empty
castawayed on a donepezil sea
and pillowed upright
thumbing to the end, again, of a dogeared bodice ripper
holy grail for the set adrift
on loan from the games lounge

you've gained weight
bloated, beached, buoyed up by chemi cocktails
Bottoms up!
in rorschach duck blot pyjamas

we're both tongue tied
you with yours too big, parrotted and swollen
tripping heavily over syllables consonants fuzzed and
memories slow spinning into softness

my words are sharp stone rattling
like the ones that scraped my knees raw
once upon a time
'you're always falling poor wee thing,' you'd whisper
kneeling beside me
as you washed my school day gashes clean

Clare Riddell

one of those sad women in books

going by my middle name
a park bench breakdown in scuffed heels
in bed at four in the afternoon
with a view of the railings

i'm not special for loving you
brushing against a fur coat fantasy
between flocked wallpaper and split leather
to wine and dine is a foolish dream

I wait for an answer
from a question never asked
cloudy eyes to match the concrete
dusty letters in cryptic code
head under the tap

so many others stare and sigh
yet I avert my gaze
in fear you'll see the wilt and decay
or worse yet
the potential

living through it

/
my flatmate says
please sort your coriander
in the fridge
it's in a bag, but the bottom layer is brown & slime
she doesn't tell me it's leaked
I find out when I lift it &
green slops up my skirt
/
an ex emails about something
reminds me
his saliva is in me
on a cellular level I didn't
consent to

my shoulders creak with his bronchitis & the
left thumb remembers punching through wall
I want to press it into the hotplate
while I cook low-fodmap lunches for the week
/
there's usually a call at midnight
time zones are shit
lines of latitude are too wide to reach hands through

we can video now which I guess is good
I blame your thin face on the filter
/
a poet told me he screams in the car when he's alone
lets it out, smashes the monotony

can't let my voice go, it'd
break my throat

/
visit a friend at his evening crematorium shift, 3 more to go
not many hours left
coz one's a baby

the coffin looks like a bedside drawer
small & white, in the corner by itself
/
some nights I want someone to hold me
against the wall with just a right hand
not say they *love* me

want to breathe   hard
forget nothing's real
fuse magnesium oxide so I can be a white flash for someone
days after I'm burnt out
/
on the straight stretch before Eureka, slow fucks are overtaken
& guys in utes do 120

there's an urge
a small twist, the Toyota steering is so light
my body would pretzel around the barrier in 5 seconds
be a mess for someone else
/
my mum used to read us bedtime stories
I'm thinking of that dumb one with the rabbits
who love each other 'thiiis' much

I want to go back to the baby in that drawer
wrap it in the lullaby jammed in my throat
/

you & I don't talk at night anymore
but I don't know if someone can actually die
if they were living
12 hours behind
/
I go to the old house
spit my loneliness into the nasturtiums & walk away

Harriet Salmon

Across the Mudflats

It will smell of mangroves
no matter how rigorously you hose yourself down at the other end.
    it will smell of mangroves in the venue
  in the car home
and in bed when you get there

  it will still smell of mangroves when you run the length of an urban beach mid-winter
  in your temperate adult city
the one too cold for them to grow.

      an empty buoy means someone is on holiday and it waits there,
   looking out to sea gentleman like a dog
the cars at a crouch on the harbour bridge
and boats in italics on the low tide.
Our curled heads climb the stone walls of halls beach
up the edge
      over the top
          marching a slog,
                    if you fall over
                      you wipe your hands on your shorts.

Dad,
  come pick me up
and take me back to our tidal beaches,
where the sea breathes in and out like a person
so everybody goes down to swim at the same time
throw me off needles eye on the inhale and leave me standing out on the sandbar
save me from work
it's never ending coda,
where five minutes with Mavis is all you get,

where the cough lozenges are the price of heating and no one opens
the curtains but you,
those twelve hour evenings with dinner balanced on the dashboard,
owing thirty grand for love of H. D. and Gil Scott-Heron
while your twenty-first birthday sits
on the edge of its seat.

Dad,
        come get me now
even from this funny town,
        I am eternally picking bits of pacific oyster out of my feet.

Friendship

Golgotha was right across the way
pret shadows thin seemed
like shadows formed on air
shades of mercury

pert translucent because miniscule
for their event like market basket
cast at dust
dragging your leggings along to it

a displaced trial monitor
chicken heads in the basket whose
forness disappears in the bright
wisp of marketing

simultaneous heave devices
sprint on the marrow
it's a spigot formula
basting like the ground is so heavy that way

fog layers without direction
letting someone know there's a light part and
something called else
partway through the thin shadow

sometimes she walks

sometimes she walks a path lined with feng trees
walks a canary in a tiered bamboo cage
walks a cat on a leash I see the Great Wall
all those steps leaving one life for another

egrets and orioles watch her cross the Plum Bridge
wave to the ferryman gather herbs beside a stone path
rescue insects stirred up by the hooves of donkeys

through the fog the call of Temple bells
there's honey in the air my daughter decorates
wax food wraps with the calligraphy of bees

paints chopsticks with wolf hair brushes
finger paints tiny poems *pale moon snowy mountains*
goldfish signs her new name 迪迪

her head is shaved her head is covered in corn sheaves
her head is bowed she wears a loose jacket and trousers
plainly woven from long-fibre cotton with a 300 thread count
and teaches the long slow movements of Tai Chi

in a teahouse she pours *conggou oolong souchong*
on Sundays she visits the grave of her new father
back home her father still faces the sea turns 70
stents diabetes glaucoma arterial vascular disease
he never gets used to it

last night I dreamt she was at the Terracotta Hospital
restoring a warrior horse the legs were in pieces
no two hooves the same with faith and patience
the horse waited to stand
will this horse bring her home?

Father Abraham

had many sons.
I am one of them —

because there's only one gender,
it's a continuum, you know,

you're just on it somewhere,
anywhere, doesn't matter where,

there's no better or worse,
the extreme left is just as bloody as the extreme right,

dexterity is just as useless as sinistrality,
all children should be forced to write with their non-dominant hand,

I say, we could all be supermen,
we're just not really trying,

hard enough, so you're on the spectrum,
who cares, it's not so circumspect,

look around, it's cool to be a spectacle,
at least you're not a spectre, right, you're a human,

you're on the spectrum,
you're one of them.

Jane Simpson

This surgery is written

in blue dye washing through a breast
in one lady in 200 going wrong —
the risk my surgeon writes upside down

in paths travelled
by isotopes migrating towards
lymph nodes

through milk ducts printing on demand
white ink, mother's tongue,
the nipple's ballpoint pen

in a title
remembered in the night
motherhood is not an abstract noun

in wire, fine as a hair
locating the tumour
two hours before

in hand holding hand
the line in my other arm
only the breast speaking

Nigel Skjellerup

Tinnitus at the Mariupol Steel Works

post-fulmination
he's left with

down-stroke bow
on A, miles long

too tenuous for air
left hand aching

for the mercy kill
but caught

between resonance
faint and deep

and the absence
of pulse; he

chooses to rise
beats waiting

for next sudden
shell crescendo

half-bodied vibrato
less of a feeling

now he's no
longer sound

Patrick

Black walls of canvas
sculptures of
every rugby player's face
in your kitchen
you captured our youth
in plaster of paris
hot Arkansas nights
tree frogs bark
women sleep naked
midnight dinners of quail
shiraz and legs running down the glass
you swirl
declare your love drunkenly
dangerous jealous women lurk
Unapologetically Australian
A handgun beside the bed
loaded for safety
Rolling Stone covers are the wallpaper
tapestry of the bathroom
black Camaro in the driveway
animal skins on the furniture
I sleep with all my senses

Chairs

Once you had to be invited to sit.
Few chairs in rooms. You stood
for more than minutes when shown in.

There was a manservant to announce you.
The master might stand near the fireplace
or sit without inviting you.

Sometimes you were several.
Only one chair near the window
which gave onto the gravel.

You looked longingly at its legs
carved like a lion's paws
its padded seat, embroidered.

You might shuffle your feet a little
when the pleasantries were over.
Chairs were a door to wine and refreshment.

If you got one it might lead to
a huge fire in the hearth
an introduction to the chair's daughter.

Strains: Citron Snacks

for Claude and Badger

Arid brown paddocks fringed with mānuka
rolled down to where the Hokianga
Harbour's protean waters vacillated hourly
between ultramarine and purple.
January sweltered to hallucination.
In a deck chair I bonged away the afternoons,
hazing-out over the pages of a gothic novel
set in an orchard near Alabama.
When I first arrived there in Ōmāpere
I befriended a local at the lookout.
He had the countenance of a great navigator —
Melanesian eyes scanning the ocean
for lost messages, the wake of ghost waka.
When he smoked a lump of your Citron Snacks
through a chipped black porcelain pipe
the cab of his Hilux filled with cookie funk,
the splash of lemon furniture cleaner.
His koha back was a bottle of Steinlager,
cold and luminous as a piece of pounamu.

Shaun Stockley

ENZED GOTHIC

there, a peel-panel hallway
lined with yawning gumboots
reserves
just the softest
fringe of light
to hang upon its mis-
matched angles
and — sickly — salt
the warm, stale air

motion is the flicker of
the ads after the rugby
the fridge light, reflected
the hesitant finger on the
bedside lamp
and the gall-green clock
ticking over
on the oven

consider the clock
it has wound its way
back into bones,
into the cracks in the
toilet window
and the long-curled edge
of a child's, or
grandchild's
school portrait
as if the curve of

long, stooped years
will scoop them back among
the bounds
of this dog-hair road

You are the reason you don't feel better

Women are bigger on the inside than they are
on the outside doctors who doubt their
capacity who constantly underestimate them
who have decided she does not have it in her
are simultaneously sure of her exaggeration
after all what do women really know of trauma or pain
they clearly do not have organs like men have
organs cannot understand the stress of winning
the bread of war or death although what is a comrade
if not a son and when she says it feels like a nine
they write six on her chart or maybe four it's a nice
round number because they know the truth when research
says they must be the same because differences are surely
only genital deep even though they clearly do not have organs
like men have organs (and after all what do women know
of trauma or pain) still this pill worked on everyone
they tested so it must be you are the reason you
don't feel better

Loren Thomas

to convince myself we're really here

We are walking through small town Japan
a mug in each of our hands.
Earl grey or a 'Janet' as you like to call it
lingers on our tongues.

It's early morning.
The neighbourhood is mostly sleeping.
You wear blue jeans, grey T-shirt tucked in,
Birkenstocks, hair in a ponytail.

I envy how well you wear simple.
I can't remember what I'm wearing.
It must be spring or autumn
One of those in-between seasons.

You are talking as you always do,
like the faucet's broken and someone
haphazardly is trying to block the spray.
I love to listen to the chaos.

You would hate it if I called you that,
chaotic, wild, any descriptor
that could indicate destruction.
It's more a projection.

The roads are narrow here.
The leaves still a cartoon green.

We walk along the river,
down the road where
the street sounds fade into forest
and the quiet could disguise

any bad intentions.
Like any moment
a hand might come from behind
and shut that faucet for good.

But all that's with us
is the occasional bee,
the first hint of dragonflies,
and the light trickle that is the river

We are walking through small town Japan
and something feels like it's ending.

home turf

Call me home, Whenua,
wipe the day from my tired brow.
Call to me your fields and wire fences.
The brakes yield to your wild-maned traffic officers.
The winding of this gravel road is a shallow imitation of the bends
of a river I have yet to bathe in

and perhaps that's why
my favourite colour is green.
Because its stitched
into every fibre
of feathery plumage
of the garment that cloaks me.

Its ragged shag of branches
gently sways in the evening cool,
silhouetted against the forest entire.
Speak to me, your ancient green karakia.

I take Te Urewera with me
to each port I visit and, in each seed,
I place shallow in the earth,
blooms there another gift of the ngahere,
another child of the mist.

If where I lost and cast to the wind
I'd hear a call, and seek the caller,
I'd turn my head and settle my gaze on the maunga.
Where the glow of patupaiarehe
begs me,
calls to me,
to long for this place.

For home.

My mother and I are more alive than either of us will admit

My mother comes to stay
the same morning
my son tells me he
'hates womens'

Write small, my mother tells me,
and so I do

not collecting but holding up.

She observes that my voice
has a rotating quality,
words get abandoned, drift
like music from a car
speeding off down the street.

My son's eyes roam across us
like bright apple buds. My mother
notices the way dawn slices
my house open at the neck,
warms the black stovetop, melts
honey into pliable food.

It is tiring, she says, how often
women ask to be loved.
Asking and asking, like the asking
is a garland, draped with a thousand
small starry knives.

I show her the new surgical scars
along my belly,
ridged, metallic red, each the length
of a single syllable.

My son asks me to butter him three
pieces of toast. He cuts them apart
with a claw mouth, hands moving
in the syrupy shape of an apology.

If you focus on the waves of light
passing through an empty room,
you will forgo the urge
to quit yourself. This was my
mother's lesson from living
all sixty-five years of her life
inside houses she always knew
she would one day leave.

tongan

with age
she becomes
increasingly desperate to
be recognised as tongan

not non-specific polynesian or
kiwi with a little bit of something
that's a very interesting name dear
but actual tongan

so tongan that rellies won't try
to show respect by seating
her on the couch with
older or pālangi relatives

so tongan that aunties will growl her
for not untying her hair at funerals
so tongan in fact that she'll
never be given a free pass

so she cultivates a tongan attitude
swears by best foods mayonnaise
and works to perfect
a teasing sense of humour

until an auntie ever-inclusive calls
her sister the tongan princess then
attempts to mend her broken heart with
and you can be the new zealand one

Which one is this?

Is this the one where every window has a crack and the third wick
on the candle won't light? Or maybe this is the one where you ignore
your own arteries but buy a plastic pump for your latest lover so you
can hand pump blood to their lips. Perhaps this is the one where the
ocean only ever looks like sky — you try to sink beneath the waves
but your mouth fills with clouds the first time you empty your chest.
I suppose this is the one where everything is blue & you're nervous to
use
line breaks
because you don't know if everyone will stay connected.

When the Light Falls from Your Eyes

He could write about anything
from the migration of godwits
to the inner workings of a pinball machine.
And still he crawled through the darkness
on hands and knees
with sparks shooting from his fingertips —
a beast in the long grass.
He could write himself into a fairytale.

Bean stalks
wrapped around their poles
reach up to the sky.

A flock of ravens
flies out
of a pizza oven.

It was hard to think
that his last meal would be served up
on a hospital tray.
There was so much left to imagine.

And in the heat of the boiler room
a blinding whiteness when someone
opened the metal door to the outside;
a whiteness that kept flooding in.

And then, on the road of whiskey-coloured rubble
(which his mother had called 'the road to ruin')
a clergyman rubbed his cold hands
and clicked his tongue, Bantu-style

before offering up a silent prayer
for the angels who were already tissue-thin
and dying among the branches of the trees.

Janet Wainscott

Life Lessons

You taught me to gauge the crimp
in a fleece, to count the grains
in an ear of wheat, to look in the mouth
of an old ewe and mark her as a cull
if her teeth were too worn
to see her through another winter.
You taught me to watch, patiently — see,
that lamb is lost, that ewe is sick, it will be
a good harvest, a bad harvest, the sheep
have staggers from the dry,
will the rain ever come, will the rain
ever stop. The sheep are newly shorn,
see how they turn their backs to the rain,
how they try to walk away
from the rain, away from shelter.
We must go out and drive them back
to the sanctuary of pine
and neatly trimmed gorse.

Strange I should grow out of the land
into words. For you it was always
the soil, the stock, the land:
lament and psalm.
Retired decades ago, you surprise me
when you say you wouldn't go farming
if you had your time again. But I can't tell
you apart from the land.

Hannah Wilson

Medusa

i meet him at athena's eighteenth birthday party,
red plastic cups swimming with poison,
a disco ball and flashing lights
mimic a ship's searchlight on the ocean.
his gaze catches on me like fishhooks.
i shouldn't have worn the colour red
and all its connotations.
blood —
that's how the sharks sniff you out
and how the fishermen reel you in.
his breath salty
condensation at my throat,
he whispers in a voice that froths with seafoam
that i am the fruit on tantalus's tree.
it is like being thrown into tartarus
but having you would be elysium
he tells me
before ramming another goblet of nectar
down my throat
olympus's finest.
he drags me to athena's bedroom
where war posters leer at me
and blu-tacked stars glow-in-the-dark
on the ceiling above athena's queen bed.
but they're stupid counterfeits,
no constellations watch over me.
i scream and scream until my throat bleeds
and the blood gurgles under my tongue.
he laughs and whispers
isn't it divine?
if i could only raise my head
i'd see a trident piercing,

penetrating me
deeper than light penetrates the sea
as the salt gets in my hair and eyes,
stings me and rubs me raw and
i realise i've been fated for this moment since pandora.
he leaves
the sheets salty and bloody
and reeking of the sea,
athena's queen bed now a sepulchre.
the door blasts open and athena
wears her fury like battle armour,
hurling her words at me deftly as a spear.
i claw at her
but my nails only close over air.
i beg her to forgive me
but she won't look me in the eye.
in me a fire blazes red as my dress,
but it flickers
with wind and storm,
and seawater chokes the flames in a single breath.
she left me all alone in darkness
but
above the cloying silence
close to my ear
i thought i heard
the friendly hiss of a snake.

nevil shute

it's september again and the smoke from my neighbour's pipe
is drifting over the fence and drowning out the birdsong
i remember when you were little and we lived in the small house
and we had no money for wood so instead we set fire to books
a town like alice was a long slow burn which maybe it deserves
i said there's a lesson in that and i warned you never to read
on the beach because although i enjoyed being in love
with the american submarine captain with the dead family
back in what used to be home it was hard not to be haunted
by the radio silence from the north and the boxes of red pills
stacked in abandoned pharmacies so that when i got older
i was surprised to emerge blinking from each decade alive
it makes one bad at forward planning i want you to stand
on the beach and not count the months october november
december before the red pills are dispatched i want you not
to know the american captain's family is like the ash from
ava gardner's cigarette gone long before you were born

Sophia Wilson

Three Parts Dis-articulated / La Désarticulation en Trois Parties

1. Talk / tongues / teeth

The truth is / glyphosate killed the bees / the hen died a violent death / he forgot German / she struggled with Mandarin / she was not born in *the year of the ox* / he was not born in *the year of the dog* / they feared contagion / they were exhausted / she spat her theeth / he bit his tongue / neither of them could afford a dentist

Parler / langues / dents

La verité c'est que / le glyphosate a tué les abeilles / la poule a subi une morte violente / il a oublié l'allemand / elle avait du mal à apprendre avec le mandarin / elle n'est pas née *l'année du boeuf* / il n'est pas né *l'année du chien* / ils craignaient la contagion / ils étaient épuisés / elle a craché des dents / il a avalé sa langue / aucun d'eux ne pouvaient se permettre un dentiste

2. Home / heart / heist

The home was / a haven / a shithole / a murder scene / every inhabitant's right / up for grabs
/ dismantled / inundated / history

Foyer / cœur / vol

Le foyer était / un refuge / un vrai taudis / une scène de crime / le droit de tous / à gagner
/ démantelé / inondé / passé

3. Land / body / lie

In time the land was / an edible garden / a sustainable garden / communal / a nature reserve / an animal rescue centre / a site of pilgrimage / a meeting ground / a dairy farm / an extracted quarry / a city / a desert / a no man's land / no person's land
In time the body was / unsustainable / non-biodegradable / irrelevant

Terre / corps / mensonge

Finalement la terre est devenue / un potager / un jardin écologique / communale / une réserve naturelle / un refuge pour animaux / un lieu de pèlerinage / un lieu de réunion / une ferme laitière / une carrière exploitée / une ville / un desert / un terrain désolé / terrain n'appartenant à personne

Finalement le corps est devenu / insoutenable / non biodégradable / hors de propos

Tim Wilson

Velvet

I never thought I'd meet you, birth father,
and so created proxies
to discard, until Ancestry.com produced a phone number.

We drive towards the sun in a borrowed Ford Festiva,
past the turnoff, past the 'Dog Bites' sign, playing tag with cloudbanks
of cancer and chemotherapy, inching forward in low gear
through the splash pad, fording an old dispute with a neighbour.

Waiting, you warn, 'Don't touch, I'm immune-compromised.'
My default is to romanticise, sorry, so I make that into a metaphor.

One of our boys resembles you at ten: cocky in portrait black and white,
as sleek as your new shotgun (small bore).
That weekend, he proclaimed, 'I'm not your butler.'

You too say things for effect. You are, and aren't, me.
Genetics: the same song reprised in flat and sharp keys.
We follow the melody
into bygones: a car sojourn through Venezuela,
helicopter gunships chopping up rebels in Irian Jaya,
the pound of rats you bought to prank a secretary
you liked, your offer to take me to
Tāhunanui beach and indicate the very spot on a sand hill
where I started . . .

    A notional location,
erosion, and the climate change you call 'weather'
having fed my history to fish. I wish . . . I wish
partly that you could do it, convey me in the Maserati SUV,
point and say, 'There, right there,'

thereby giving me licence to walk
an earth I didn't really touch until your grandsons were born.

Adoption, what used to be called 'illegitimacy'
(the disease, once, of more) is a perverse amnesia,
remembering what you'll never fully know.
Shadows lengthen. The hills here on Abel Tasman's
periphery are dark
by afternoon tea. Black ravines extend like the keys of a piano
that seizes fingers, and won't let go.
Clustered on the slopes, unapproachable deer
munch; indifferent, noble:
waiting to be eaten. Your quad bike plays 'Für Elise'
back to the mansion.

I don't remember you in Sydney, an apprentice roughneck,
the year I was born in Dunedin, before
your wife and children, I mean, other children intervened.
A few years later you and they would live
around the corner from our church, manse,
and book-lined study on Devon Street, New Plymouth.

Once, as a present, my Dad rented seats
in a Cessna. We flew through the sun, a droning seagull
peeling the breeze to buzz a rig, Penrod 73,
where you were performing alchemy.

He built me a fort of packing crates. Through gun ports
my school friends and I fusilladed Wehrmacht brigades,
cartoon Nazis who screamed, 'Donner und Blitzen!'

On Sundays, at 9 p.m., we listened to the *Goon*
Show, oblivious to the headless doe seated at the Kawai baby grand,
tapping out a Captain & Tennille refrain.
Love will keep us together.
Love will tear us apart, again.

I've come to believe everything has meaning,
even me.

            It's not your fault.
Deer, by the way, moult: embroideries of pelt
litter the paddock we're standing in. Romantic, sentimentalist,
bastard, I press a tuft to my jacket pocket.
We talk around your diagnosis, tumours in triplicate.
You tug. Forelock falls to gumboot.
'It's supposed to do that,' you note, 'Chemo's poison.'

Driving back out of the sun, I blink.
How are we so old, and still alive? Is this an orison?
During the following weeks, as thoughtlessly as you helped create me,
my hand will travel to that pocket, dispersing serrated, white-tipped
filaments
to render my eft-pos card unreadable, to cling, skeleton-fingered,
around Wilfie's bottle,
to impersonate centipedes swarming my desk. Much of this actually
happened, and is bearable.
Later, Google will confide that deer shed hair anticipating spring,
the time when what's new becomes true again.

Hiruhārama

As for the spot: definitely
Not that place up the river —
I'd hate that
— J. C. Sturm

The convent's roofline stamps the sky
above the carpark: a cross, a chimney.

Narrow steps hewn in the slope,
a thin handrail. Long grass, buttercups.

A glimpse as we climb of the river
sliding broad and brown below. The car

cools and ticks, the ear adjusts.
Inside, it's as expected: simple, spare.

+

A cabinet holds sufficient crockery; a shelf
a water jug. Teapot, table, straight-backed

chairs. The mataī boards are swept. Barefoot
we pad from room to room, through rooms

bone-clean, as clean as graveyard bone, hollow
as the space inside the bone when marrow's gone

to dust, through rooms you might call empty
were they not (the word arrives beneath the roof

in the gallery of green and liquid light
that is the dormitory) *abundant*. The single beds

in rows, the austere coverlets, the rib-stark
crucifixes. Plain, and yet this plenitude,

the work of windows, mullion-crossed, positioned
on the unlined walls like works of art. Fern fronds

fill the frames. A ponga arch, a horse. Still
life, it seems, a fine and beautiful arrangement.

+

Grit, a sticky burr, an insect — something —
snags the horse's tail. It flicks. Nothing ever

stops and we are in the current. Pure
with rage a woman's voice streaks

across the valley. *Get in here!*
You're gonna get a hiding!

+

Truth, that fuse. Worn blankets,
winter-frozen feet. The sleeping space

tips and ripples. The bones are brought
to light. Not so much abundant, now I see,

as *thorough.*

+

Hers is the voice I take
from Jerusalem, ringing like a bell. Down

from the dormitory *get in here* to the bench
and the bucket and the bending and the tub

you're gonna get you're gonna get

to the suds and the sheets and the piss
and the shit and the spit and the sweat

and the semen and whenua blood and the mud
and out into the garden of blue-sashed virgins

with accepting hands

+

hers is the howl
I pack in the car and take to the road

a hiding a hiding but can't take away:
hers is the scouring love-cry that goes on

shimmering in that place between the cross
and the chimney, above the buttercups, over the river.

Chantelle Xiong

Aged

Gradient blue turns white, black.
I can almost drown — my head and heart, barely afloat.
Can I run on water?
Can separated chain links still hold me up?
One big happy family.
The lemon rots in the fruit bowl.
Fungi grows at the roots of an old oak.
Poison never looked so beautiful, a ripe cherry red.
I trudge through damp leaves.
Droplets of water collect on the single strand of spiderweb.
Elegance.
It tears the throat of its prey,
I bleed out quickly
Ramariopsis pulchella, a threatened species.
An invited guest never felt so foreign.
Sunset terrain
Lined up in a wine cellar.
I watch as we drive past 228.
Alone or at home?
Two sides of one card.
A heart in a deck of diamonds.
To feel or to value.
So much beauty in a waterfall so deadly.
Carried me to a calm lake
Skinned me for the boat.
I beg to ask who will enjoy the view.
I turn to page one-one-five.
I'm suffocating in these polluted clouds.
Have I lit a fire?

Essays

John Geraets

these are my eyes: Michele Leggott's poetry

The volume *Mirabile Dictu* celebrates Michele Leggott's tenure as poet laureate (2007–09) and marks an inflexion point in her poetic career. In brief, the volume presents a world of adaptation: coming and going, joining and severing, isolation and community. While the poetic remake is remarkable, a major achievement, it also involves an intriguing, at times tricky, endeavour to reconcile the poet's experience of being pulled in two directions — on the one hand towards deepening everyday personal intimacies and on the other towards a revered, creative communitarianism. The call to synchronicity in the face of these pulls is the focus of this essay.

such an engagement[1]

We begin at Leggott's return from Vancouver in 1985 with a PhD (subsequently published as *Reading Zukofsky's* 80 Flowers by Johns Hopkins University Press, 1989), the near onset of a debilitating eyesight condition,[2] and a plan to renovate the Aotearoan literary dwelling house, especially for women's poetry.[3] Some 20 years later, the laureate's tokotoko (talking stick) provides further support, conferring mana and authority to speak in fronting the ongoing journey, something that no doubt continues following Leggott's recent retirement as professor of English at the University of Auckland.[4]

Her ascent begins immediately.[5] Leggott features in the 1988 anthology *Yellow Pencils: Contemporary Poetry by New Zealand Women*, with her poetic front room already aesthetically filled with snapshot flowers, carefully named and brightly coloured:

> bright   clean   particular
> but nothing hard about it
>
> Just the way things go

fuchsias
wine-dark (there it is)
in a blue . . .
('Yellow Pencil')[6]

and then
more comes
    Prune plums bloom
    blue in the leaves
bloom
    prunus
    spaces
('Rose 7', *Yellow Pencils*)

The formative verse is visually precise, rhapsodic, and derivative enough stylistically to serve as due homage to modernists Louis Zukofsky and William Carlos Williams. Already, the radical *Parallax, And, Splash, Antic* (New Zealand's first feminist literary culture magazines, conceived in the image of its immediate uber-male predecessors) have largely run their course, and Leggott's significant first appearances are in Dudding's mainstream *Islands*, followed by *Yellow Pencils* and, also in 1988, her first book *Like This?*[7]

The next volume *Swimmers, Dancers* (1991) consolidates the early rise. One key poem asks 'why are the roses (which aren't / even here) suddenly twisting // into circles? Why are we drawn / to these figures' ('Oldest and Most Loyal American Friend'); another echoes the title of her 456-page tome *Reading Zukofsky's* 80 Flowers —

in the style of leaves growing
eyes curving
towards the question just where do the roses swing
are they pink and blown and warm as sleep
at the gate where lavender works the bees all year round
or red and sweet as tea grown cool because everyone went to check

some story about the *wind roses* you already knew were lining the nest
with scent and bloom and two quarter-view profiles
flickering out of the frame

— while another pleasingly stretches page margins to left and right ('Merylyn or Tile Slide or Melete'). Before going on to explore imaginatively vaster constellations, from *Mirable Dictu* onwards, we note that the formative work resonates with discrete sensuous details in which flowers and circles predominate ('Rose' associations abound).[8]

find home . . . dark / within daylight
('18')

the immaculate shape of things to come
('learning')

a mystical etymology
('lebh', *DIA*, 1994)

the daughters of light, what are their qualities?
unsapphirine unsilvered mirror of where I am
('hyle', *as far as I can see*, 1999)

Through the 1990s, formal experimentation advances, including pictographs that take the shape of circles ('Tigers' in *Swimmers, Dancers*) and pursed lips (*DIA*).[9] *as far as I can see* includes an early instance of Steinian paragraphing (the undulant 'a woman, a rose, and what has it to do with her or they with one another?') and proclaims the encroaching *unseeing* of failing eyesight as the adopted poetic condition. Henceforth, a more deeply integrated enquiry evolves. The poetic gaze becomes fervently '*Angelike*' (see '*Persica*') and the scope of work extends into celebration of a creative community in the form of an imaginal elect.

Mezzaluna

Mezzaluna, selected poems (2020) jumps forward two decades and allows a retrospective tracking of the entire trajectory. Initially published by Wesleyan University Press, then again locally, it's dedicated to 'those who travel light and lift darkness'.[10] The experience represented increasingly encompasses acts of memory and the former pithy versification gives way to protracted lyrical ruminations, frequently arranged in sequences that utilise longer lines, or paragraph formats, akin to the admired Stein's practice.[11]

On the way through, there is much to encounter. Historical associations serve as a means for glass-of-divination insights into what really matters. Leggott retraces footsteps of family members past and present, introduces us to personal and artistic friends and associates, to literary tourism art history geography anthropology botany meteorology biography local landmarks flora and fauna,[12] as well as the occasional foray into literary modernism.[13] It's an expansive, precisely delineated world.

But beyond recalled familial and historical attributes — and of more particular interest to this essay — is the extent to which there is a fundamental realignment in personal and poetic identity, until the two merge. The facticity of the past, respected without any sacrificing of verisimilitudinal rigour, serves as a springboard to transform facts into living relationships. In fact, verisimilitude and transformation prove mutually reinforcing. While movement towards the sought horizon of light is unswerving, an inflexion occurs whereby an increasingly restricted visual range necessitates — and spurs — a developing inner transformation, away from image-making based on visual quanta and towards image-making as constellational, self-rejuvenating.

Visionary repossession, as re-seeing, loosens time and distance constraints and promotes human renovation. For Leggott, memory empowers repeated incursions into the bleak but unavoidable desolation of Hades, recasting moments of despair into portals of light.[14] This constitutes her sublime mythos, a luminous rhapsody.

lacunae: trajectories

Mirabile Dictu heralds retrieval. Commemorative, it restrains the previous inclination to libidinal sensuousness, while expanding the geographical and thematic range. The *miracle* is that sight should occur not so much in a *seeing through* (overt spirituality has little truck for Leggott) as in extending sight beyond the merely visual. *Dictu* urges us to partake in associations re-realised, intimacies restored: 'one thing leads to another / though the trail is not always / obvious'. Disparate events superpose in a way that allows a tunnel-holing between them ('*visible invisible*'), just as sightlessness drills through to serendipity. Even the fabled rose, brightly ornamental earlier, reappears now as past's *inshine*: 'Rosa rubiginosa / the sweet briar   a bramble / dug up and replanted by historians' ('the liberty of parrots'). The — now increased to six — senses are reified in a sensualised mindscape, whereby earthly existence is reclaimed in a form of synaesthesia:

> why are these details
> compelling   if not because
> the gift [wild rose] moves between its preservers
> who are also vulnerable
> and parts of the same story
> ('the Darwin lecture')

As 'parts of the same story', world and art coincide: 'the great work / of recombination' ('teatro della limonaia'), whereby 'the circle is not a zero' ('il mantello / the cloak'). The equals sign points both ways, where 'magic and tragedy / took the stage together'; where, more tellingly, personal heartbreak (the poetry hints at many instances) is greeted with the same graciousness as are everyday pleasantries (ditto). Nothing *self-avails*. The trick is transformation; and ultimate configurative power resides in imaginal creativity, whether individual or in confraternity.

Prior to the retinitis diagnosis, physical seeing held sway. One delight — but also a painful irony — is that the loss of sight is compensated for by the capacity to re-see as re-imagination. Literally, like unsighted Milton or Borges, or figuratively, like banished Ovid or Dante, being outcast provides a pretext for reconciling blighted latitudes of vision. Leggott's journeyings (up north, Australia, North America, Italy, Portugal) are secular pilgrimages, accompanied by fellow-adherents, visiting blessed destinations, observing rituals. A feeling of palpable joy (the poet's middle name) irrupts everywhere:

> The library at Alexandria burns
> but my heart is a pool where the white birds step
> among incipient papyri.
> ('ladies mile', *DIA*)

proprioception

To this point, what has been written is broadly explicatory. Now I wish to examine more closely the workings of what I have termed Leggott's imaginal, by focusing on her most recent single volume, and to my mind her finest, *Vanishing Points* (2017). The eight sections comprise standalone yet structurally interrelated poetic-biographical vignettes. For example, the second section, 'Self-portrait: Still Life. A Family Story', cites Elizabeth Eastmond's essay on artworks by Frances Hodgkins and an account written by Martin Edmond tracking Colin McCahon's conjectured movements during a wander across Sydney as 'starting points': these two unrelated sources are actually used to explore 'the conditions of family creativity' that includes Leggott's artist father and mother (the latter's 1960s artworks are analysed in substantial detail).

The eighth and final section, 'Figures in the Distance', does something similar in another time-tunnelling scene that incorporates prestigious modernists, including Stein, Pound and Williams, as the poet's extended family. As always, the research is meticulous, and the material world and the language in which it is represented are regarded as wholly dependable, inviolable.[15] As dark and topsy-turvy as the world remains, only shared imaginal endeavour retains the capacity to keep righting it.

The opening section, 'The Looking Glass', makes this clear. Leggott is with close friends Susan and Leigh Davis, the latter suffering from advanced aphasia.[16] 'Radiance' is the distinguishing feature, resolutely grounded while seeping through the words:

> bright events
> in every part of the sky except the radiant
> music in my heart
> ('horologium / the clock')

Leigh Davis appears as 'L' in (imagined) dialogue with 'M', or alternatively as his doppelgänger 'Macoute', the name imprinted on the impressive flag-hanging that decorates the Davis property at Matapōuri[17] (and an interesting variation on the 'Willis coyote' self-characterisation in his first book of poems, *Willy's Gazette*, 1983). In contrast, 'Figures in the Distance' sees Leggott share a dance with a sprawling modernist crowd (this time in paragraph format):

> Who are these like stars appearing? They are my cliffs and I am going home. Who are these of dazzling brightness? They are my people and I bring them with me.[18]
> ('21')

One touching vignette in 'Figures in the Distance' has beloved guide-dog Olive interrupt everybody in the middle of 'the Modern Poetry class' when she starts to lap water from her bowl. In this consilient world, a spontaneous connection occurs with another famous writer, whose own dog, Basket, proved time and again a treasured companion — the priestess of modernist poetry, Gertrude Stein:

> This is as good as listening to her one-two-three one-two-three lapping at the water bowl, threes and fives, fives and threes, before I remember

> Gertrude Stein's little dog and what listening to the rhythm of his water drinking taught her about the difference between sentences and paragraphs. That paragraphs are emotional and that sentences are not.[19]
> ('12')

The lapping sound and vocal rhythm of the prose are synchronous with the sentiment articulated. In the following paragraph, we have corroborated what we now well recognise as Leggott's abiding vision:

> Transforming consciousness, transforming art, transforming the image. The apparition of these faces in the crowd. Transforming language, transforming the self, transforming the city. I will show you fear in a handful of dust. Transforming myth . . .[20]
> ('13')

As I have emphasised, language serves for Leggott as a trustworthy instrument of retrieval, providing a means to realise relational depth and steadfastness of virtue. 'The Looking Glass' — a surprising exclusion from *Mezzaluna*, perhaps because (at least to my mind) the language tends to be more abstract and indeterminable, at its least-reliable, something Leggott is usually careful to avoid — is my personal favourite, employing wit, non sequitur, irresolution, gnomic utterance: 'she starts around the ecliptic as they chant / in a ring' ('circinus / the compass'):

> M: What was it teaching us?
> L: Poetics.
> M: Are you sure about that?
> L: It could have been 2.30.
> ('norma / the square')

> when the holes in the card line up
> with constellations drawn by an unnamed lady
> starlight falls precisely on human eyes

looking into Urania's mirror.
('columba / the dove')

As a way of seeing, the sequence gives fulsome tribute to a close friend and fellow poet. We observe moments of plain-spoken intimacy — surfacing, resubmerging — among other cryptic exchanges (reflecting Davis's aphasic condition). Simplicity and complexity merge in wairua, abidingly deep accord:

raining in my heart ever since we've been
apart   the parabola of his hands above his
open mouth and the shout of something that could be
joy or another outburst of pain.
('horologium / the clock')[21]

This is Leggott at her finest: nuanced, warm, incisive. It also takes us, and Leggott herself, to the outer reach of her language use. Strangely, it reveals an element of jeopardy, in that it highlights her implacable allegiance to language as a fundamentally straightforward storehouse of meaningfulness. It is the modernist's dilemma. How is such meaningfulness to be retained in the face of Davis's incoherent utterances? Is he saying something different in the very discombobulation of his words? How does language operate outside the norms of accepted conventions?

Perhaps unwittingly, 'The Looking Glass' reveals what's at stake in Leggott's valorising poetic. Elsewhere, especially when there is less immediate interaction between persona and subject, the felt insistence on implicit value in the material can become wearying. This occurs in *Heartland* (2014), in the retracing of Lola Ridge's footsteps through downtown Sydney and in the recounted incidents involving family ancestors and First World War Europe. Similarly, the vivacious travelogues in *Journey to Portugal* (2007) and through *Mirabile Dictu*'s Italy leave a feeling that something more is being asked of the contents than is intrinsically there.

Even in the present volume, while beautifully constructed, 'The Fascicles' and 'Emily and Her Sisters', in their conflating of hereditary with artistic virtues, leave the reader feeling they are sewn into the same fabric. In such cases, the imaginal becomes insistent, narrowed in possibilities.[22]

The pulling in two directions I mentioned in opening relates to this valorising strain. The lure of the light means that certain poetic and experiential elements are either relegated or entirely bypassed, within an enduring brightness. Despite life trauma bravely faced, the poet's and that of others, the true-to-life persona deliberates nowhere long on gruesome details or human negativity, whether disillusion, disappointment, irritation, understandable exhaustion, or plain fury. Commendable in itself, and something there is no wish to gainsay, the aligning of virtuosity with virtue does introduce some non-negligible aesthetic risk.

Buoyancy in performance tends to repress the unintended, anything whimsical or funny — anything, in the end, falling short of implicit commendation, including self-commendation. The downside is that tonal range and variousness in personae are inhibited. Perhaps this is why I like 'The Looking Glass' so much, because there's an actual questioning and answering back. This is not to say that having a univocal poetic temperament is not an acceptable delimiting stance to take for a poet whose foremost aspiration is to establish harmonic correspondences. Ultimately it is something that each reader will find their own response to.

'Figures in the Distance' provides, in this respect, an interesting blend of the pull between direct sympathetic encounter and idealised community. The notes list 27 modernist luminaries, 'and anyone else I might have missed inadvertently'. Together they form a visionary troupe that walks 'towards a blackout that seems perpetually delayed'. Shifts in attention are navigated via use of Leggott's long preferred direction-finding apparatus — 'the compass rose with its 32 points . . . going round in circles', a beautiful structural conceit.[23]

Thirty-two well-contoured paragraphs, in contrast to the dissonance recorded in 'The Looking Glass', play to Leggott's strength of pellucid woven configuration. The ostensible guide is Stein, although here, as elsewhere, it is really Pound, with his lifelong campaign to secure poetry's perpetual newsworthiness ('What thou lov'st well is thy true heritage'), who is the prevailing mentor. In fealty, we have Leggott's 'Rise up and play every day for the oral and intangible masterpieces of humanity' — and, again — 'Transforming history, transforming America, transforming modernism'.

Stein is emulated or, in this instance, too-closely echoed — but what shines through and matters more is Leggott's limpidity of style:

> A white rose. See. A white rose stencil. There. A white rose stencilled on asphalt. Marking. A white rose stencilled on the footpath. Dividing. A white rose stencilled on the footpath to show juncture. Or continuation. ('5')

Juncture. Or continuation? The latter is obliged to absorb the former, eliding the full stop that stands between them. The light shines through or encircles obstacles, eventually engulfing them. This is not to depreciate the light, or Leggott's sharing of it, rather it concerns the legitimate purposes to which poetry is directed. We hover somewhere between Stein's deathbed 'What is the question?' and Keats's 'Beauty is truth, truth beauty'.

The truest moments are those of unfettered affection, for family and relatives, for Olive, for Davis, for the pantheon of creative high-achievers, a preponderance of them women. With this consideration in mind, and in closing the circle on the misgivings I have mentioned, we might well leave a last word to Leggott, looking forward to receiving the next turn in the story, wherever it may lead (or join):

> When [the dog of tears] reaches her she will bring her eyes down to look at the ruined city and become blind. Everyone else will have their eyes back. She will have the dog of tears. The dog of tears will bark holes in the last page of the book and lead her through one of them. There they

are, the dog of tears and the woman who wept. His nails click on the rough stones. She who can no longer see begins to tell a story.
('30')

---

1 Leggot is the author of 10 poetry titles (1988–2020), plus a contribution as editor in several other texts, including *Big Smoke* (2000), an anthology defining 1960–75 literary culture; a couple of books on Hyde, plus, more recently, New Zealand-raised poet Lola Ridge (2019). Leggott continues to be highly regarded among contemporary USA writers and critics, as evidenced by the Wesleyan University Press imprimatur accorded *Mezzaluna* (2020) and the Jack Ross-convened retirement tribute, *A Birthday Festschrift for Michele Joy Leggott* (October 2021). Other achievements include establishing the NZ Electronic Poetry Centre (nzepc), modelled on similar digital archives founded by Charles Bernstein and others at Buffalo and the University of Pennsylvania (PennSound). Recipient of the Prime Minister's Award (2013), Fellow of the Royal Society of New Zealand in 2017, Leggott continues to live on Auckland's North Shore in Devonport, a cherisher of family stories and her immediate surroundings.

2 *Retinitis pigmentosa* is a genetic disorder of the eyes, generally gradual in onset, that causes loss of vision. Symptoms include trouble seeing at night and decreased peripheral vision, with possible tunnel vision

3 The feminist house trope is pertinent. Riemke Ensing's *Private Gardens* (1977) provides a rickety foundation. Living space extends in Wevers' *Yellow Pencils* (1988), a more substantial collection. Bringing us to the present, Paula Green's *Wild Honey: An Anthology of Women's Poetry* (2019) literally bursts with rooms and passageways, through which some 200 women poets are — literally — paraded. Leggott's assault on the Curnow et al. 'androcentric' legacy is announced in *DIA* (1994) and critically extrapolated in 'Opening the Archive: Robin Hyde, Eileen Duggan and the Persistence of Record', included in *Opening the Book*, edited by Mark Williams and Michele Leggott (1995), pages 266–93. As an aside, there is a counterargument to Leggott's, percipient as it is, in the strongly male-supported career trajectories of the two poets mentioned above, as well as other women poets including Ursula Bethell, Glenda Rawlinson, Ruth Dallas and Janet Frame. Nowadays, the literary space is arguably dominated by women.

4 The obvious grandee of the previous generation is C. K. Stead. His retirement from the University of Auckland English Department in 1986 coincides with the year of Leggott's employment. Much the same can be observed of Allen Curnow, two generations prior, feminist arch-nemesis (retired: 1976). Revisionism is intrinsic to local journeying narratives.

5 A first handful of poems was published in 1980 by Judi Stout, poetry editor of the student newspaper *Craccum*, when the two were working at the University of Auckland general library.

6 Inadvertently, editor Lydia Wevers doubles the 'l' in Michelle in her introduction, while deliberately multiplying the anthology title to *Pencils*, as if to say all contributors share the newcomer's unique attribute. For her part, Leggott determinedly avoids unintendedness, at times overly so.

7 Leggott was in Canada from August 1980 until November 1985. She missed the rise of the new magazines, although she managed to get a copy of Leigh Davis's *Willy's Gazette*.

8 Rose is accorded various significances, tropological as well as topological: a plant, family names, an eatery, the name of a seagoing vessel and the heartfelt, romance in general, literary likings, and our own mundane *Rosa rubiginosa*, in botanical fact a 'restricted environmental weed'. As Stein unforgettably says, 'A rose is a rose is a rose' (meaning: a rose is never simply a rose). It goes without saying that Leggott's image-palate habitually inclines to the generic rather than to particularising detail.

9 Tellingly, *as far as I can see* carries notes on the back cover, proffering an unguarded confidence: 'I am losing my eyesight to a condition called retinitis pigmentosa. It is the sound of words in darkness, and the words in light. But eyesight is not vision.' In *DIA*, the trope remains notional: 'Have you seen they ask, the rose in the steel dust? . . . Femina, femina, that would not be dragged into paradise . . . O taste and see; chew, swallow, and transform'.

10 The title is crafty: the explicit reference is to the crescent-shaped steel blade used to cut cooking ingredients; more suggestively, *mezza* pertains to time, while *luna* depicts a moon shape: *Cutting with the moon?*

11 'I am not interested in the one-page poem unless it is a constituent of something bigger.' In the same note in *DIA*, Leggott self-identifies as a kind of historically investigative ventriloquist lyricist (the sobriquet is mine).

12 In the maturing writing, botanical taxonomy branches out (so to speak), with dollops of juxtaposed post-laureateship Māori/Latin to supplement the usually preferred French and Italian interpolations, spanning as well a wider range of named local trees and shrubs, especially bird life (kingfisher/kōtare, woodpigeon/kererū, fantail/pīwakawaka , morepork/ruru). 'The wedding party' ('Coda', *Mezzaluna*) uses Māori and Latin excerpts taken from *The Richmond-Atkinson Papers* (1960), Leggott claiming for them 'their common ground' in the Taranaki War, 1860.

13 Among those, local and overseas, inducted into 'Figures in the Distance': 'Rita Angus, Hugo Ball, Christian Bök, Jorge Luis Borges, Pam Brown, Alan Brunton, T. S. Eliot, James and Robin Fryer, Ida Gaskin, Mary Gauthier, Ernest Hemingway, Lila Hobson

and Meadows Rendel, James Joyce, Tessa Laird, David Lees, Federico García Lorca, Ern Malley, Pablo Neruda, Ezra Pound, Marcel Proust, José Saramago, Gertrude Stein, William Carlos Williams, Virginia Woolf, Dorothy Wordsworth'.

14 Benightedness — whether in the form of blindness or banishment, or our own deserted-by-language Leigh Davis – is often considered part and parcel of the poet's lot. Borges' epigraph to 'Self-portrait: still life. A family story' says, 'since I have lost my beloved world of appearances, I must create something else'. Leggott makes of disability her strength: 'into the abyss / from which we will emerge shining' ('listening', *Heartland*).

15 Several poems are based on painstaking research by a posse of research assistants: 'Other key images are six works by ['the sister of my great-great-grandfather'] Emily Harris in the collection at Puke Ariki (one for each of her sisters) . . . Thanks to Anna Boswell, Makyla Curtis, Bronwyn Lloyd and Erena Shingade for their generous contributions to the project'. Historical events include: 'Work for the living' (a road trip north to Tūwhare's tangi), 'olive' (Pike River mine disaster), 'The Fascicles' (Taranaki wars), 'Wind and Weather' (wreck of SS *Gairloch*), 'after the war', 'bombardier' (WWI). Ruminative travelogues take in much of the Western world. Routinely, snippets from other writers are merged into Leggott's texts, homage as internal pilgrimage. A prominent example, 'Blue Irises' in *DIA*, includes scraps taken from Fleur Adcock, Ursula Bethell, Eileen Duggan, Bernadette Hall, Dinah Hawken and Robin Hyde (*Mezzaluna*, notes).

16 The sequence was written 2012–13, following Davis's death in 2009, and he is at once a real and a ghostly presence in the sequence. The intermittent question and answer sections are miniature dramatic scripts.

17 The letters are sewn on both sides of the flag, which produces mirror-writing on the reverse side.

18 The voice in the poem belongs to Ida Gaskin, an English teacher at New Plymouth Girls' High School, where Leggott attended. Gaskin adored T. S. Eliot and introduced his work to students. The old hymn lines were previously sampled in 'The Fascicles' (email from Leggott).

19 'Olive was deployed each year to lap water and be recorded for the class so that we could test Stein's assertions about rhythm. It was a great way to start the class on *Tender Buttons*. Much hilarity' (email from Leggott). Gertrude Stein and Alice Toklas had three canine Baskets in succession, perhaps another inadvertent connection to 'one-two-three'?

20 The transformations refer to the 12 lectures of English 216, Modernist Transformations, taught by Helen Sword and Leggott (2014–21). While Stein is an important figure for Leggott, the truer guide is perhaps Pound, whose imagist poem is alluded to, and whose principle of *logopoeia*, whereby unrelated events resonate

deeply in the mind, applies crucially to Leggott. His *melopoeia* (sound-correlates) and *phanopoeia* (image-correlates), apply no less. Interestingly, the original version of 'In a Station of the Metro' (*Poetry*, April 1913) utilises the same blank spaces frequently employed by Leggott as scansion markers.

21 I understand the reference in this poem is to the two buddha figures resident at the back of the boatshed (email and conversation with Susan Davis, November 2021), the second of which adopts such a posture. However, I associate it also with Leigh: a black-and-white photograph featured in an obituary notice shows him in a polo-neck reclining in a deckchair, looped arms ('parabola') cupped behind his head, his mouth slightly agape (*ἀγάπη*).

22 A case in point is the pivotal role given the steamer SS *Gairloch* in *Heartland*. Featured pictorially on the cover and dominating the end 'note', sailing logs also feature in italicised sub-text in 'wind and weather', a sequence commemorating voyages taken by her great-grandparents. Serendipitously, as children, she and her siblings would 'trek at low tide across acres of boulders to where the rusted iron ribs of a wreck heaved up against the sky' — SS *Gairloch*!

23 The compass recurs as navigational — and imaginal — device. Whether in the tokotoko form or other vessels of locomotion, the world travelled is the whole that encircles one. The rose is a kind of circle, and references to circles abound. *DIA* includes a sequence title that shows the 'L' contained within the actual word's shape. 'The Looking Glass' appeals to a children's circle game, the circle itself, the eye as circle, with pieces headed 'Pyxis Nautica' (nautical compass), and 'compass rose'.

Shaynah Jackson and Heidi Rogers

Triumphantly Queer: A conversation

The university gingko dangle the last of their brilliant yellow against a pristine mid-winter blue. It's easy to forget you're on campus when the air hits your lungs as though fresh off a snowy mountain. There's vigour in the collective mood. It seems everyone is greeting Shaynah as she approaches a small circular table outside Kahurangi Café, coffee in one hand, her copy of *Out Here: An Anthology of Takatāpui and LGBTQIA+ Writers from Aotearoa* in the other. The hues in her burnt-orange coat and beanie are complemented by a brighter shade of lipstick, highlighting the warmth in her smile. Her vibe flows in alignment with the crisp day — sleek and shining.

Opposite, Heidi pulls out a chair and checks her crotch-zip is behaving itself. So far, so good, though her leggings are riding up, exposing hairy ankles above 'barefoot' sneakers — their recycled plastic stained a rustic palette of sand and dirt. Feeling somewhat overexposed after months of hermiting, she smooths her mess of self-cut curls — which are beginning to look suspiciously like a mullet — and takes another swig of peppermint tea, while a man with a guitar sings 'Polly Wolly Doodle' and café-goers chitter-chatter under a moistening sun.

The two brunettes shift their focus from talk of PhDs to the two identical covers between them, flowing rich with colour. A queer anthology, such as this, they agree, warrants a queer review, and what better way to achieve this than between a couple of queers, spilling the tea . . . ?

What follows is a conversation between Heidi Rogers and Shaynah Jackson, concerning their reading of *Out Here.*

Shaynah: So, lovely co-reviewer, what are your initial thoughts on this anthology? How far through are you, and how did you broach reading this impressive text?

Heidi: Ha, good question! My approach has been rather higgledy-piggledy. I found I could attend to each piece better if I opened at random and let my mood be my guide. There really is something for every mood in this anthology. I have both ugly-cried *and* laughed out loud — luxuriating in the glory of authentic queer shenanigans. I have felt the stir of vicarious arousal (so hot); and seethed, while simultaneously experiencing vindication through each writer's willingness to name the things we are taught to keep silent. Some pieces sprang out and punched me in the guts, leaving me stunned by my own ignorance; others soothed me in the middle of the night (lit by smartphone torch, casting mighty shadows over the ceiling). I frequently felt the tingle of shared understanding or precious new insight.

For example, Jessica Niurangi Mary Maclean's piece, 'Kāore e wehi tōku kiri ki te taraongaonga; my skin does not fear the nettle', masterfully interweaves history and culture through a lens I had not encountered before. I was so captivated, I barely breathed throughout my reading. By her last word, I was imagining how different life may have been for everyone in Aotearoa, if, instead of imposing Western patriarchy and homophobia on tangata whenua, my Pākehā forebears had adopted te ao Māori's reverent attitudes towards women, children and queers.

As I leaned into the complex swirl of emotion that comes from facing up to the consequences of colonisation, while also being a product of colonisation, I felt a selfish grief in knowing that my predecessors suffered at the hands of toxic masculinity, despite living in close proximity to a worldview that held feminised peoples in high esteem. In this land, there was an alternative to my forebears' tradition of gendered subjugation and oppression. We could have done a lot better, sooner.

After reading, I phoned my dad to debrief, and together we marvelled at the power of the written word to bring about perceptual shifts.

So, to answer your question — I have found this has been an utterly dynamic interaction! What about you, how was your first encounter?

Shaynah: We broached the text in slightly different ways, which surprises me none. I was more typical in my approach and read the anthology from cover to cover, interested in how the arrangement by alphabetised first name would pan out (spoiler: well). I too found that every mood was housed in one story or another; I certainly went through the motions, in the very best way. This was an aspect that appealed to me most about this anthology: there was no unitary or overarching queer story. Instead the gritty and triumphant both featured. The multitudes contained, within its pages as well as within Aotearoa's queer community more broadly, are celebrated in fullness, the rainbow in technicolour.

Did you notice any specific themes or aspects of this text that stood out to you?

Heidi: Mmm — rainbow in technicolour — I like it. What stood out most was my hunger. My compulsion to get stuck in. I can relate to what the editors, Chris Tse and Emma Barnes, observe about growing up without queer visibility. It's there, but I'm frequently left unsatisfied by the junk-food quality of pop culture representation, which often lacks diversity and complexity. As you say, our community has a myriad ways of being, and our lives have meaning beyond coming out.

When I became a 'baby-gay' at 29, I was starving for the stories and poems contained in this anthology. It is the free-range, organic chicken-soup-for-the-queer-soul (or butternut for the vegans), with way more spice and grit. I am intrigued by how the writers can take everyday life and somehow make it simultaneously more beautiful and obscene. In her poem, 'I AM SO IN LOVE WITH YOU I WANT TO LIE DOWN IN THE MIDDLE OF A MAJOR PUBLIC INTERSECTION AND CRY', Hera Lindsay Bird writes:

> it's like
> you've finally found someone that interests you
> and you get more and more interested
> like a fascinating disease

This was my experience with *Out Here*, and my interest was contagious. I read the aforementioned poem to my partner, who promptly commandeered my copy of the anthology and only returned it after taking photos of it to send to her friends. 'I usually hate love poems,' she said, 'but I love this.'

Does that answer your question? Was there a particular theme you were drawn to? I'd also like to hear your thoughts on the environmental embeddedness of the text, and how you feel this selection is relevant to queers living in Aotearoa in the early 2020s.

Shaynah: Oh, I could not agree more with the necessity (the joy! the triumph!) of seeing oneself represented in these pages. In the process of notetaking, I penned this note in response to Carolyn DeCarlo's 'Equilibrium of a Rigid Body', which I think does well to show just how joyous this representation can be:

> I am charmed to see mention of Hamilton Gardens, cheers Carolyn DeCarlo. The Hamilton Gardens serve as keeper of my most formative lesbian embraces — the secrets of my coming whole — and your nod to my beloved, absurd little home did not go amiss. And so it goes with *Out Here* that one can find themselves, apparent and unashamed, within the fold. That one can encounter their own memories writ large, this is to say writ proud, couched within the electric-pink covers, tucked in and kissed goodnight. Here we find ourselves safe and sound.

This is a far cry from, as you say, the junk-food representation we're oft fed — here's looking at you, corporate-moguls-turned-pride-advocates-come-June. This anthology does not censor its queers; it does not privilege a well-behaved, assimilated or redemptive kind of queerness. Featured instead are the unashamed desires of queer love, of sex workers, of city dykes, and of the BDSM-enthused. Non-conformists and hedonists alike frequent these pages, as they should.

It is a delight to read queerness not as an effort toward assimilation, but as a celebration of the myriad desires not neatly designated conventional. In its willingness to share stories of queerness as a disruptive, exhilarating and erotic force, this anthology is a triumph.

As Hera Lindsay Bird writes:

> It's a great stupidity to waste your life on right-seeming behaviour
> Like putting a coin in a jukebox that only plays whale song

I was resolved to fold the corner of every page of this anthology that stood out to me, and before long I had folded nearly every page. This is no surprise to me, of course. In these queer writings I find that tinge of coveted vitality: pages at once deeply personal and yet so true to my own experience. I want to wrap myself up in it as though a blanket to warm from the cold. I want to curate myself a safe nest of these remarkable writerly things and settle down for the winter.

In response to your question, my notes on the celebration of a queer counterpublic, or a queer refusal to oblige a unitary way of being, relates to why I think this anthology is so important for contemporary queer readers in Aotearoa. I remember negotiating my own sexuality in my late teens and concluding that I could show the world that, *in spite of my queerness*, I could be successful and impressive and a good daughter and all the rubbish thoughts that my younger self hadn't the good sense to unpack.

But I wish I had had something like this to show me that my own queerness was not something I needed to compensate for, and that my life did not need to be dictated by arbitrary qualifiers of good and impressive — *and normal.* I could be, as Heather McPherson writes:

> An aged dyke in a ditch
> A broomstick witch
>
> whose eternity is
> to stretch into plaiting
> just-dropped petals as linings
> for pliant rose-nests exuding
> hundreds of dusk-smeared
> scents.

For its readers, this anthology is a conjuring: a heady cauldron calling forth our desires, demanding that our wishes be granted. It is a magic of our own making, an almanac. This is a spellbook to be coveted and studied, passed down for generations; contained in its covers is a magic ready to spill over and change the world.

And filtered through the poetic is a homage to those remarkable stalwarts of queer, like Leslie Feinberg and Gertrude Stein, a gesture to the occurrence of queer beyond our isolated NZ-selves. And thus, throughout the pages of *Out Here*, I am reminded of belonging, I can recognise myself as part of the collective tissue — a body at once local, global and timeless.

Did you feel the overwhelm of reviewing such brilliant writers? I had a moment of wondering if I could do justice to these pages!

Heidi: Wowee, I'm rather dazzled by all these sentiments imbued with witches and dykes in ditches! Yes. First, I share your wish for teenage-Shaynah. Teen-Heidi could have done with these stories to contradict her internalised queer-phobia, not to mention society's imposed simplistic notion of gender. I rue the day I plucked my lush pre-teen 'stache, after being mocked by the backyard rugby boys (I ditched the game after said boys refused to tackle me, despite the fact I could still smash them into the dirt, even with ovaries and breasts). One of the most unsettling aspects of coming out queer, I think, is not knowing who is safe to be yourself around.

You mentioned the deeply personal aspect of this anthology. I appreciate the vulnerability expressed within the triumph — as you so aptly put it. I don't need to see another writer burying their gays or using our gender identities and sexualities as trauma-porn. I do need to see more queer voices reclaiming queer trauma.

I needed to see Hinemoana Baker's 'rope'. I needed to see Semira Davis's 'Hiding'. I needed to see Stacey Teague's 'Angelhood'. I needed to see Vanessa Mei Crofskey's 'Peanuts Pickled in Aged Vinegar'. I needed to see Oscar Upperton's 'Small talk'. I needed to see all the contributors take up space, unapologetically (and it was a thrill to flick through and observe how each unique shaping of black and white spaces has collectively created a dynamic work of visual art).

There is something incredibly healing about witnessing queer people reclaim — through narrative — power which has been stolen. It gives me goosebumps just thinking about it. So, if I may share your metaphorical blanket, Shaynah, I will seek refuge from this deeply traumatised world for a second, slow my breath, and quietly hold all that is difficult to process. For I feel these pages offer a safe place to start processing together. To feel into that global interconnectedness you speak of, and find glimmers of hope, as we time-travel back to the beginning, and imagine possible futures (see, for example, A. J. Fitzwater's 'Offset').

In considering your final question, I am reminded of the first time I witnessed essa may ranapiri perform. Until then, I was unaware a poet could wield 'the force'. I remember watching in awe as they brought forth — from bright red lips — this 'queer magic' you speak of, and deftly took command of all the energy in the room, lifting it to the most euphoric crescendo of collective queerness I had ever observed.

When I opened the cover of *Out Here,* seeing their name put me back in that awe-inspired state. And yes, if anyone other than Dr Tracey Slaughter had asked me to participate in this review, I would have gone with my gut instinct and run away.

'What do I know about poetry? Who am I to comment?' were thoughts that picketed my brain. However, I believe effective writing lures understanding on an embodied level, without necessitating a particular set of knowledge. In other words, if a piece of writing makes me *feel* something, I believe we have interacted meaningfully.

I send my gratitude across the ethers to all the people who shared their treasures with us. The sheer opulence of feeling and meaning conjured through this work of art has been an honour and a privilege to behold. Thank you.

Shaynah: I, too, send massive thanks to the writers included in this anthology, what a privilege to behold indeed! And to the editors responsible for curating this work, of course, without whom we would not be privy to this exquisite assortment.

As a final note, I just want to echo your earlier statement regarding the theme of climate crisis throughout this anthology. Remarkably, the frank truth of climate disaster reads less as existential doom and gloom — though this would be a fair response — and more as an imperative: to live now, to be joyfully queer *now*. As Pasan Jayasinghe writes:

> Impermanence is the fate of queers. It is especially pronounced here . . . Everything — the law, society, our own shame — conspires the future out of our hands. All that remains instead is the present. In that, you think a kiss is enough. It has to be

The present belongs to us, to the unruly and triumphant, to the keepers of queer stories. In its command to be remarkably and radically queer, this anthology is a provocation and a liberation.

Reviews

Aimee-Jane Anderson-O'Connor

Oscar Upperton

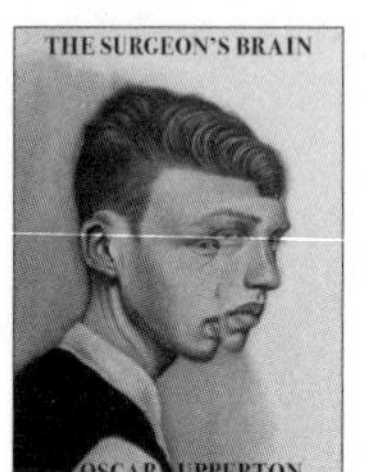

Oscar Upperton
The Surgeon's Brain
Te Herenga Waka University Press, 2022
RRP $25, 96pp

In the opening pages of Oscar Upperton's 2020 debut collection *New Transgender Blockbusters*, the speaker muses on the potential of resurrection, and the transformations which such an endeavour requires:

> The dead should come back changed,
> or what's the point?
> ('Door against the cold')

This exploration of resurrection and its implications threads through Upperton's 2022 collection *The Surgeon's Brain*, a verse biography centred on the life and times of surgeon and transgender man Dr James Barry. The collection operates both as a life story and as a reflection of the processes of writing the lives of the dead.

The book is loaded with metatextual observations, which wink to us from the page and call us to consider the intervention of the poet in this telling, observations that take on extra affect as the poet's job is placed alongside the work of the surgeon. Upperton highlights themes of inheritance and connection: 'To sketch the bones of the hand requires the use of a hand'.

In the poem 'Dissection', the use of the poetic first-person voice again affords a space where the poet and his subject are drawn into close communion. Barry's questions are simultaneously those of the poet, and, as we read, ours, too: 'What do the dead think?'; 'What do the dead feel?'; 'What are the dead good for?'. These are, in many ways, the main questions underpinning this collection. The next lines provide a compelling response:

> There is a religious answer, but we are men of science
> and would say the dead are to be learned from.

Yes, Upperton invites us to learn from the past and the processes of revisiting it, but this collection is by no means a merely cerebral exercise in metatext. This is poetry which insists on the sensory. *The Surgeon's Brain* is a space of imagination and surreal play, and it is also a space which brings the material conditions of the Victorian era into close attention. Here we rub shoulders with the past and its physicality: muddy and tactile, pulped and bloody. Here, stifling rooms packed with the ill; here, paint chips on a windowsill; here, smoke, shutters. These material conditions are, of course, political, a fact the poet explores with subtlety and nuance. This is work with a stethoscope pressed to the human heart, and Upperton is a poet with a finely tuned ear for the pulse of class, gender and power.

The imagery in this collection is striking, at times ruthlessly realistic and at others dreamily surreal. Upperton has a stunning poetic range, taking us from floating gossamer imagery of 'innumerable silver spiders', to the present-participle pull of 'Blistering, cupping, copious venesection'. There is a real fluidity in this collection, and while each poem stands alone as a masterclass in rendering a moment with devoted attention, the collection also operates as a satisfying and engaging whole.

This is the collection of a poet who has totally hit his stride.

Aimee-Jane Anderson-O'Connor

Tim Grgec

Tim Grgec
All Tito's Children
Te Herenga Waka University Press, 2021
RRP $25, 96pp

Tim Grgec's debut collection *All Tito's Children* explores the life and legacy of Marshal Tito, the communist dictator of Yugoslavia. The collection is loosely based on the experiences of Grgec's grandparents, who escaped Yugoslavia in the 1950s, and it draws on extensive research. At the back of the book, Grgec details the many historical sources he consulted, including a number of prose biographies; however, this book lives beyond this existing corpus.

Indeed, Grgec revels in poetic licence, and treats his historical figure with openness and, at times, even playfulness. This verse biography takes the Cold War era, rife with secrets and suspicion, and treats it with warmth and curiosity. *All Tito's Children* is a collage of sorts, made up of enticing fragments: samples of local folktale and myth, imagined and redacted letters, family recipes, acts of a play (incomplete but with character lists), and snippets of the 1953 Constitution of the Socialist Federal Republic of Yugoslavia.

Family relationships provide the anchor and emotional centre of this collection, casting historical moments into close personal relief. I am drawn especially to the imagined story of siblings Stjepan and Elizabeta, and their shifting understandings of the almost-mythic figure of Tito. Grgec's use of the game in which the children try to trick one another by telling two truths and one lie is an endearing image, and a metaphor for the poet's art, too. We get to join the children in questioning the stories we are presented and we join them in leaning close and listening hard.

Grgec makes effective use of white space, gesturing to the gaps and uncertainties that plague the archives of Tito's life, and echoing themes of censorship. He has an immense skill: keeping questions circulating, resisting easy answers or the urge to flatten or oversimplify. In Grgec's hands, history is an open book, and biography — as in the fragmented biography in the fifth section of this collection — is much more usefully a constellation of stories and facts than a simple or singular line from birth to death.

The lines are voice-driven, clear and declarative, and his imagery is carefully chosen, even shocking in its often-understated directness. 'A single candle' lights the table at which a mother recounts the sound of a man begging for his life. Here and elsewhere, the collection registers the horror of the war that preceded Tito's appointment as prime minister of Yugoslavia:

> Snow was
> thawing across the battlefields, enough that the hands of the dead
> soldiers could be seen reaching upwards.
> ('Stjepan')

This, and the recurring imagery of chickens and willow straw, stayed with me for days after closing the book. I am left, too, with a firm understanding that any conclusions I might be tempted to make about the figures in this book are unsteady, one of many possible readings.

All Tito's Children had me reaching to know more about the history of Yugoslavia. Much more than that, though, it has me reaching for more of Grgec's work, and eagerly awaiting what comes next from this exciting poet.

Elizabeth Morton

Elizabeth Morton
Naming the Beasts
Otago University Press, 2022
RRP $25, 96pp

Elizabeth Morton does not flinch, does not look away from the flicker or the flame, the wreck or the still-curling smoke. *Naming the Beasts* collects a menagerie of her finest works yet, prowling and pressing against the glass pane of the page. But any sense of division between us and the page is notional. There is intimacy in her use of address throughout. Morton often evokes a first-person speaker, who 'write[s] something confessional on the glass', who is open with her fear and want. Elsewhere, Morton addresses the reader directly, using the second person 'you'. We do not escape the poet's pen. This collection had me shuffling in my seat, unsettled.

Indeed, there is little stillness in this book. The opening poem, 'Feral', sets us in motion, leaving a party 'carrying only heat'. Throughout the collection, we have the sense of being hunted by loss, haunted by grief and the full-body ache of absence. There is an ever-pressing sense of impending and an already unfolding cataclysm. We are warned:

> Everything is hot and waiting
> to ambush you from the sedges. *Knock knock.*
> ('Road trip with my adolescent self')

This is a poet unafraid to speak right to us, to ask big questions of us, to spit it straight, 'say it real', to speak with a 'gumline of gravel'. Her lines are kaleidoscopic, like broken glass or gutter glitter. Full lines stack detail, and Morton's skill for striking simile and extended and recurring metaphor combine to mark the surreal and uncanny in the familiar and everyday. This is poetry in full flight, fight, curl and claw, and its creatures are loaded with heat. Morton watches for ignition, and this collection is lit with gunpowder and brushfires, 'ash-cut stiltgrasses', campfires and kerosene, sparklers burnt right down to the wire.

The language is lush, at times beyond my vocabulary, but the sounds and textures carry me through and invite me to test language out in my body for sense. This is not a book to be swallowed in one sitting: it demands attention, and I read it one poem at a time, carrying its images with me through my days.

The connection between lives and their surroundings is a key theme throughout, and Morton brings settings to vivid life, finding the animal in the most unlikely places. Juxtapositions crackle: the domestic and the wild, the woods and the city, the private and the public, the doomed and the hopeful. There are also surprising images, striking in their pairing: plums and the spice girls, heatwaves and nectarines, bitumen and sorrow.

It's a collection with more questions than answers, holding space for uncertainty and wonder. It lends us permission to move beyond the known or the say-able and to howl to the wide open, to each other. It invites us to come together, speaking with a voice that asks us to meet them 'in the dog-tender night'. The signature Morton heartbeat knocks through the collection, the pulse of another beast ready to walk beside us.

Jenny Powell

Jenny Powell
Meeting Rita
Cold Hub Press, 2021
RRP $27.50, 80pp

Jenny Powell's 2021 verse-biography collection *Meeting Rita* foregrounds the relationship between the poet and her subject, and invites us to encounter New Zealand artist Rita Angus with the same warmth that pours from the poet. The opening poem, 'Meeting Rita', brings Angus and Powell face to face, sharing space and even wearing matching coats — coats which serve as an evocative metaphor for the local landscape:

> Corrugations of hills
> folded
> into our sleeves, tumbled
> to the flat plains of cuffs.
>
> Coats stripped of scrub,
> of border protection
> between out and in,
> we faced each other.

Landscapes weave through the poems in this collection, which at times take the form of vividly imagined ekphrasis. As with Angus's paintings, Powell presents carefully balanced, often spare lines, which leave space for voice and breath to circulate. It is luminous with this light, and dazzles with its attention to colour. The poet's palette captures 'weak sun-spill', a 'sea-blue frock' and the 'Gold-tinged roam of hills'. It is a prism through which Angus's light shines.

However, it also transcends this existing oeuvre, and comprises something entirely new. *Meeting Rita* is an imaginative feat and is propelled by the connections between Powell and her subject. The opening poem, and its 'coats stripped of scrub' also speaks to the examination — and often dissolution — of the borders between these two figures.

Powell seizes on the tools of poetic licence, creating an 'if-only world' in which the two meet, creating an opportunity to directly address Angus with playfulness and offers Angus insights and retrospect beyond her original contexts. In the poem 'Central Otago', the poet's questions, though unanswered, create a sense of intimacy and allow us to imagine a space in which Angus might answer.

Indeed, much of this collection's work lies in this liminal space which the poet names 'Between Two Worlds', and it is this space to which the poet returns Angus in the penultimate poem of the collection.

Yes, this book is rich with light and life, but there is suffering and loss in these pages, too. Powell is a poet in full command of her subject, and she guides us to difficult terrain. Some poems in this collection gave me a sense of wide-open space and lungfuls of air, while others took my breath away. 'Echocardiogram' and 'Fog on a Sumner Street', 'Painting Over the Underground', 'The Sunny Side of Electroconvulsive Therapy' left me breathless.

There is pain here — lurch and cut, hobble and moult — the flurry of fear and desperate survival. As in the poem 'Watercolour', there are moments where the light cannot touch. These moments are, however, never overdone, and Powell's use of punctuating stops, short lines and stilted line breaks create small poems which pack a punch. This balance is powerful, and only adds to the tender-shock and ache of these poems.

I am a long-time fan of Powell, and this latest instalment continues my indebtedness to her for a big part of my love for Aotearoa New Zealand poetry. *Meeting Rita* is a masterclass, the collection of a poet in perfect control and communion with her craft and subject.

Frances Samuel

Frances Samuel
Museum
Te Herenga Waka University Press, 2022
RRP $25, 88pp

> So it's better you are now inside the glass
> rather than outside looking in.
> Because inside the glass box of the museum
> the idea is that everything we love survives.
> ('Essential Tremor')

Museum, Frances Samuel's second book, is a collection that weaves in and out of display cases. One moment, it lives outside of its glass boxes, observing from a remove the curiosities and tiny tragedies unfolding within. The next, the glass shatters, the words become intimate and flayed; 'a poet explodes at a kitchen table' and later takes you 'walking through my veins on the scenic route'.

This collection contains three sections — super(natural) world, (im)material world, and object lessons — which are stitched together, bound by an eclectic array of objects: by breath and babies, ghosts and skeletons. Moments of the comically absurd — chickens refusing to wear their trousers — blend into soft loss, as in 'How to Catch and Manufacture Ghosts'. Humour and death intertwine with the small magic and traumas of the mundane: 'tiny nicks in the fingers, held breath —' and native bees, 'humming, not whispering, their tongues too short for the introduced flowers'.

The impersonal becomes the site of the personal. These pieces reflect on moments of a life as the boundaries between material/immaterial and real/imaginary are increasingly collapsed. The static everyday and the shifting unknown are destabilised, made hopeful and dangerous by a fresh curiosity. *Museum* is a collection invested in questions and what-ifs:

> What happens when the objects of memory no longer exist?
> What's it like to be always night?
> When will the robots come?
> ('Robotics')

Beneath these questions there is an ongoing tension, ebbing and growing between pieces. A sense of 'the sudden lightness of a loss that has been coming for a long time', building to moments of combustion. This museum is a heart: stocked with the recognisable, yet, at its centre, 'a black hole in the floor the lighting technician refuses to spotlight'. It is here that the poet runs to and where we must as well, evading security and 'leaping like your life depends on it'.

Joanna Preston

Joanna Preston
tumble
Otago University Press, 2021
RRP $27.50, 88pp

The second poetry collection from Joanna Preston and winner of the Mary and Peter Biggs Award for Poetry at the 2022 Ockham New Zealand Book Awards, *tumble* is a collection that burns and spirals, freefalling from 'words that trail like broken wings' in 'Lucifer in Las Vegas' to the 'Fallen stars, like shards of glass, scattered through your hair' of 'Lost'; combusting in 'Fare' beneath 'an ember etched into the very fabric of the air'.

tumble contains three parts and is bookended with portraits of women — 'Female, nude' and 'Nightfall' — which shiver easy perceptions of femininity and the female body. From the first piece, 'Female, nude,' replicated here in full, there is a delightfully unexpected juxtaposition of the delicate with the dangerous:

> The things we prize. Innocence,
> the sleeping fire that speaks
>
> through the long white flower
> of her spine, the curve
>
> of her hips the rim of a slow
> turning wheel
>
> on which to break a man.

The first section of *tumble* begins to draw into question commonly accepted narratives, offering body and voice to the fallen, those in the shadows and the 'blood-song of the desert' living in 'reflex twitch' 'beneath the fear of wings'. Pieces such as 'Portrait of Great-Aunt Lavinia as a bathysphere', who 'crossed gladly, slipped into the boundless kingdom of the ocean leaving nothing but her name, a story touched with brine' unearth the hidden, give chest to whispers, refuse to turn away.

The second section is a wintry mourning, mouthing loss 'with the quiet voice of snow'. These pieces sink and sift through the echoes as 'None of us leaves anything but traces'. Opening with 'Lijessenthoek' in 'the fields of Flanders — rich red of the cemetery gates', this is a journey through the cautious hauntings of trauma in 'A body, blind and deaf to itself', searching for footing at a party of gods where 'When I couldn't breathe they said I sounded sexy'. It closes with 'The Ministry of Sorrow', a monument to be built 'for all we have lost, for all our losses to come'.

In part three, we are dropped into a place of burning, of the unheimlich, the uncanny world of 'Fare'; 'a night for slinking cats, and taxi drivers', where cities crumble and resurface among memories 'burned into my skin' by the ember of 'a long, red hair'. These pages are a croon of longing, of paramours crisped to ash and shadow; of 'full-bellied moon and howl' where matches flare 'like a curse, like a hole ripped open into another world'.

tumble is carefully constructed of:

> So many threads, our stories, braided
> and tasseled or tucked neatly into the backing —
> ('Lares and penates')

An empowerment, a ground steadily shifting, a question: Who has the power to push, the power to leave, to burn, to break? To fall, to fly, or to hold back the weight?

Jessie Burnette

Janet Newman

Janet Newman
Unseasoned Campaigner
Otago University Press, 2021
RRP $27.50, 106pp

I will say it died the way
calves wrenched off their mothers
sometimes do,

telling the truth of things,
knowing the difference
between enough and too much.
('Good intentions')

Unseasoned Campaigner, the debut collection from award-winning poet Janet Newman, sways the line of 'enough and too much', glancing unflinchingly between the beauty and tragedy of the cattle farm: the poison runoff and the sweetness of 'warm breath on your skin [. . .] until you send them on their way to be killed'. This is a collection that swings hard and lands heavy, closing lines a poignant brutality on the intake of a breath. *Unseasoned Campaigner* is grounded in farmland, in 'a sky so blue and hard you could skate on it', never flinching from the things we do or the things caught in the crossfire.

Section one, 'How now?', offers an honest look at the road from the pasture to the meat-processing plant where cattle 'walk toward imaginary fields' and 'the only prayer is the shush of water'. This section culminates in death, by slaughterhouse and by disease, in an ultimate rejection of the 'rope around his neck' but the inevitable loss of 'singular cattleness'. Two pieces, 'Ode to Mycoplasma bovis' and 'Anti-pastoral: Biosecurity Act 1992, section 130', particularly resonate during our current time. Cows in quarantine, 'at least two metres apart to ensure there is no touching, no nose to nose contact, no exchange of breath' acquires a new meaning in the time of Covid-19, troubling easy boundaries between animal and human.

Section two, 'Tender', is a loving portrait of a father, traced with gentleness while retaining the sharp honesty of 'How Now?'. The pieces in this section echo wartime in the mundane brutality of farm life, as warm family memories ripple into those of violence, where 'words wilted our petal ears, hung like ghosts with all the dead in the living room'. These pieces pulse with person and longing. The father in 'Man of few words', whose 'language is electric rhythm of pump and wire', and the mother found in 'the slow stretch of dough, the sure way the air was caught', are affixed to the page against the affront of a drought of memory and rain.

Newman shows these figures to us in flashes, at times in harsh, meticulous detail, and at others with the feather-light destruction of pieces such as 'Drought', 'Next day', and 'Father's beanie', the closing poem of section two, replicated below in full.

Limp as
a shot hare,

pilled, frayed,
oil-stained brim,

loose ends
of stitch.

In 'Ruahine', the final section, we find a recovery and a readjustment, sinking into well-trod memory changed as 'I came to be the one to decide where to dig and when to fill in'. This is a section contemplative of what it is to 'be' in a place, and how that shifts across time and generations. For the first time, the collection moves beyond the farm to the sea, where 'the words you wanted to say' fade into 'miles of driftwood on the beach'. New memories become the site of longing as children grow and come into their own, so that 'even loss has its own joy'. We close with the sublime in 'Ruahine', 'low hills around the old woman range clutching the purple spill of her skirt'; the contrast of regrets and the 'vacant bedrooms' of children grown, with the beauty remaining: 'To see the hills across the bare land. To see them rise up so strong and clear'.

Vaughan Rapatahana

Vaughan Rapatahana
mō taku tama
Kilmog Press, 2022
RRP $38.50, 32pp

What is a reviewer to do with a book of poetry of deep and single-minded grief? Firstly, and practically, it can be described. *mō taku tama* (for my son) is a collection of 15 poems written 'over several years in response to the suicide of my loved son, Blake, in October 2005'. The writer's driving forces are that he 'cannot cease writing about Blake', and that 'in this way, I keep him alive'. There is a photo of Blake.

The titles speak consistently: 'last time', 'talking to my son in a funeral home', 'lines on loss', 'for a dead son, six years on', 'I should have done more', etc. The poems are mostly in English; several are in te reo Māori with English versions attached. All of Rapatahana's battery of sparky, experimental and unorthodox orthography, vocabulary, spacing, lines, fonts and layouts is at work, marshalled for effect both by their presence and by their absence.

Secondly, the contents can be made clear and illustrated, without intrusion or value-judgements. There is achingly missing human correspondence: a father and son 'as aleatory aliens', 'flesh & blood / in name only / genetic synchronicity / but NO / common language / other than obligatory chitchat'. There is event-memory: 'last time / together / we seldom spoke / until / I bought / us / pies / in / Tolaga'. There is regret and responsibility: 'we should have / said more / on / that trip', 'I spoke more authentically / to you / during those / thirty / etiolated minutes / than / I ever did / when you were alive'. And there is raging despair and unrelenting sorrow: 'brush away / those tears', ‘gutted still’, ‘shit of a way to / leave / us / son’.

Slight and occasional breaths of spiritual communication and quiet appear: ‘the zephyr that is my dead son / wafts sometimes right through me’, ‘this was your favourite verse/something I did not know / until later / far too late’. But mostly it is unceasing despair and guilt: ‘infernal bells’, ‘pervading death’, ‘hells eddies’, atrophic brains, early shrouds, the kōrero never had, the mokopuna never shared, fissure, disillusion, the ‘endgame dive’, vultures, bandit-pirates, catafalques, and tears.

This is a powerful, heart-wrenching and deeply moving book. To make this judgement requires justification — a ‘thirdly’: some assessment of the book’s/the writing’s undoubted quality and value. To intrude into such poems is not easy.

Third, then, achievement can be reckoned, not by ‘literary criticism’ but by the evidence of like company. In the canon of the poetry of grief, works such as Donne’s ‘A nocturnall upon S. Lucies day, Being the shortest day’, Shelley’s ‘Adonais’, Tennyson’s ‘In Memoriam’ (or parts of it, at least) and Ted Hughes’s ‘Birthday Letters’ can stand as benchmarks, or companion pieces. Each is different in object and in style: but none of these is a Sympathy Card — there is no hiding (despite some of Tennyson’s protestations) from raw grief and horror in ideas of God, Heaven, or some earth-lingering shade of comfort, that give neat social acceptance to despair in the form of a well-behaved balance of proper sorrow and proper consolation, in equally neat verse.

Why does a likely reader of such a book as *mō taku tama* value the terrors of honesty? Because the writing is personal, and true, and neither the poet nor the poems bow down to any kind of attitude or expression, closure or philosophy, of the ‘till we meet again’ and ‘an angel is watching over you’ sort. They are the cry of a human being who cannot ‘behave’, and, importantly, *worded to match*, and so have all the power of individual mind, thought, emotion, expression, independence, and the vital spark of freedom that makes us worthwhile, and such poetry worth reading.

Closure?

The world's whole sap is sunke:
The generall balme th'hydroptique earth hath drunk,
Whither, as to the beds-feet, life is shrunk,
Dead and enterr'd; yet all these seeme to laugh,
Compar'd to mee, who am their Epitaph.
(Donne, 'A nocturnal upon St Lucy's Day')

Heaven?

. . . oh, dream not that the amorous Deep
Will yet restore him to the vital air;
Death feeds on his mute voice, and laughs at our despair.
(Shelley, 'A dream of the unknown')

Consolation?

A hand that can be clasp'd no more —
Behold me, for I cannot sleep,
And like a guilty thing I creep
At earliest morning to the door.

He is not here; but far away
The noise of life begins again,
And ghastly tho' the drizzling rain
On the bald street breaks the blank day.
(Tennyson, 'Dark house, by which once more I stand')

Diminution, even?

Not very clear grey, made out of mist and smudge,
This thing has a fine fuse, less a fuse
than a wavelength attuned, an electronic detonator
To what lies in your grave inside us.

And how that explosion would hurt
Is not just an idea of horror but a flash of fine sweat
Over the skin surface, a bracing of nerves
For something that has already happened.
(Hughes, 'A Short Film')

In this company, Vaughan Rapatahana's *mō taku tama* belongs (whereabouts is for the reader to decide, if it matters, and should they want to), occupying a place among the poems of the brave and desperately hurt, who cry out in their own voice in ways that move us, and, yes, keep the dead alive.

Blake

[me tangi, ka pā ko te mate i te marama — let us weep, for his is not the death of the moon]
it's ten years now
& still you escape me.

as your sister births her son
I have only photos of mine;

            they
st utt er here   and   there
       a c r o s s our
stoic walls,
like an affliction
                &
they are all liars,

a pastiche of
the days you
conspired to outrace me,
overdrink me,

elude me,
the absent father.

it's ten years now;

as I last saw you —

that brute room,
that ignorant coffin
& that f a r a w a y stance

in your eyes.

Vaughan Rapatahana

Vaughan Rapatahana
ināianei / now
Cyberwit, 2021
RRP $25, 172pp

When you buy this book, prepare to be positively discomforted: that is to say, deeply and gainfully put out of your way. The persistent layers of pain, anger and love; the delights and despairs of known and exploited places; the fury of historical injustice; the mingled tenderness and analytics of emotions and ideas; and, not least, the questioning and explorations of ways of writing, the use of te reo in a world stupidly dominated by English — all make this a collection to challenge and change a reader.

The contents, as hinted above, are divided into four: ngā whakawhanaungatanga/relationships, ngā wāhi/places, te hitori rāua ko ngā aituā o tēnei whenua/the history and tragedies of this land, and ngā aurongo rāua ko ngā huatau/emotions and ideas. It is a welcome structure: the intensity of thoughts and feelings, the demanding play of dark and light, the dual-texting of te reo and English in many poems, and the typographic and pictorial added-extras only gain in effect from the ordering, flexible as it may be.

In 'relationships', many in dual-text, the poems concern the desperate pain of a lost son, friendly and merrily militant new neighbours, love in lockdown and the death of friends. Much of this is almost unbearably moving, and some smilingly getting-on: from 'no primogeniture' and 'as I lose another' to 'the new neighbours' and 'a lexicon of love'. The language (I refer here, as I must, to the English versions of all the poems, provided by Rapatahana himself in every case: how else do you tell the people who have marginalised your culture and your language what they have done, and continue to do?) bounces and flips from invention to deep gravity, the vocabulary and layouts unsettling and, as far as they might be, un-English.

> the house
> was a whale carcass,
> filleted
>   flotsam
>   & jetsam
>   here
>   where
> there   &   any ^
>
> upside the corrugated
> tornado
> that was once a roof
> he acclaimed us
> every time,
> 'kia ora ki te whānau' —
> his smile
> an effulgent salutation,
> his tattooed wave
> of hammer,
> a benediction.
> ('the new neighbours')

'hey fantail' comes with a photograph, 'knitting a poem' with some knitting hints, and 'went to the urupā' with a Māori proverb. But it is the searing pain of the 'Blake' poems, a constant in Vaughan Rapatahana's work, that burns the reader's sensibilities. I believe it is necessary to read these poems complete, and in dual-text where written so, and I make no apologies for not quoting and displaying pieces of them.

'places' features 'july in pampanga' (a Philippines home), Aotearoa's mountains, lakes and bays, and 'kerikeri — our town, their bullshit'.

Visits to Parihaka and Mangakino provoke the gentle melancholy of known and loved places undergoing 'development' and 'progress'. The Kerikeri poem encapsulates the lot — wonderfully. Beginning with a misguided 'white person's' patronising depiction of Māori in the car parks and shops of the place, stuffing their faces, smoking, playing video games and shopping for 'staples', Rapatahana asks that we listen to 'the huia bird / listen to the voice of truth', and continues, in exasperated plainness, as if explaining the obvious to someone who cannot see it:

> the indigenous people of the kerikeri district
> choose how they want to live
> when they want to
> where they want to;
> not like this fantasy.
>
> it's time to get real for some white people.
> real like the original inhabitants of this town.

This takes us connectedly into 'the history and tragedies of this land'. Here, the tone is less explanatory and kindly: with good reason (reasons all provided). The slaughters of Māori at Ōrākau (1864) ('does anyone know what happened there? / does anyone care? most cars zoom past myopic / while those sparsely parked there / are all-too-often mere / mobile phone cockpits'), the appalling social statistics ('after Christchurch') concerning Māori suicides, domestic violence and child maltreatment, climate change, the Waikato wars, an encounter with a citizen antagonistic to the flying of the 'standard of Aotearoa' ('but that is not New Zealand's flag') all add up to a devastating re-look at the way things are in a country so often regarded as God's Own. Rapatahana merely wants the truth:

it is my job
to write about the past
and the many bad events;
that face this intense darkness:
the real void.
('the void')

The last section, 'emotions and ideas', is perhaps the most various, but nonetheless compelling and concentrated for that. Poems of 'the virus', swans on a lake, thoughts of death ('I need to welcome him / before he strikes me unawares'), on always speaking your own language, books, the act of writing, generous love, using the word 'fuck', and, near the end, an 'epiphany', make for a rollercoaster ride of thought and feeling.

This is a book of poetry that should not be missed by anyone who thinks they know what poetry is and does. Vaughan Rapatahana is unique and challenging: to ignore what is here is to deny poetry its roles as agitator, experimenter and criticiser; and to miss out on expressions of love, death, despair and kindness that, though seen as usual contents of a book of poems, are not done in The Usual Way.

It is tempting to end a review with the shining contentment of 'an epiphany today' ('my brain now a calm lake'): but that would be too conventional, perhaps too English. Try this instead:

most of my words concern
cloven people.
the schismatic sh at te r ings
their bro ken souls,
the arcane stretchings
of orphic texts
their flailing hopes,
& the convolute repeats
their involute habits.

the body of my work
                                        is an urupā
remote & elusory.
feel free to
discover,
drop in & delve,

never forgetting
to sp i r i n k l e
                              your wairua
each time
you clasp shut
the cover.
('most my books')

Maryana Garcia

Cadence Chung

Cadence Chung
Anomalia
We Are Babies, 2022
RRP $25, 64pp

If one day, long after the twinkling lights of our time have gone out, intellectual explorers from some far, far away civilisation land on Earth to find out how we once lived here, I hope they find Cadence Chung's *Anomalia*, preferably encased in glass and vacuum-sealed.

Once they release *Anomalia* from its protected state, I hope those readers of the future will find in it wonder and reality, faith and reason, emotion and logic, science and art, fact and poetry.

From the collection's opening poem, 'abstract', I was glued to the gaps between each line. I wanted 'The scientific journal / with findings whole and mealy' in my mouth. I was fascinated by the juxtaposition between 'not a single skin has been left untouched' and the imagery in 'every flesh gets culled sooner or later'.

Having 'abstract' lead into *Anomalia* was like making a promise. These poems are not just a toe-dip, they are a full-on skinny-dip into the deep, sometimes turbulent, waters of Chung's imagination and experiences. Through 'abstract's lines, it feels as if Chung is warning the reader: I will reveal to you the 'gossamer thread of life' by slow and careful 'vivisection'. The rest of the collection not only fulfils these promises but also saturates the reader's expectations.

Anomalia combines science at its most analytically attentive with poetry's hardest hits and warmest embraces. The result is a contemplatively structured debut collection that is both poetic science and scientific poetry: an honest study of life.

In 'dawn chorus' Chung meditates on the cries of cicadas and elevates them into something hymnal because 'a life is a life is a life', and is therefore praiseworthy. Then she brings us down to gritty earth by reminding her readers how 'the fields that poets / wrote sonnets about / were damp and mushy and slick with ants'. The muddy fields become even more heroic for being ant-slick while cicada song, usually a background hum, is raised to the level of Delphic oracle.

Then 'rise' illustrates the dualism of being human by pointing out that while we 'are all soft animals, poked and prodded', we can also 'shake off the amber / and fly out of the museum doors'. Again, Chung takes an objective observation, a fact put poetically, and then turns it into the stuff of dreams.

At its most pinch-real, *Anomalia* seems to me to be the subtle, long-grown fruit of looking hard, hearing loud, smelling deep, tasting strong and feeling wholly. There is no other explanation for the way Chung wields words with precise verve so that each poem is infused with the kind of energy readers will feel down to their atoms.

One poem which really shook me to my core was 'magnum opus':

> There will be a moment where you'll wonder if you've reached your best point or your worst and maybe it all means something but all you can think about are the toothpaste stains and the lemons painted on the mirror frame because all you can really think about are details . . .

The vulnerable mundane and the existential meet in everyday life. How often have we asked questions of our own reflections? The difference with Chung is that she has posed her questions like a scientist and communicated them as a poet. She has pinned fleeting thoughts to hard board and put them on display. In revealing herself, she has revealed us to ourselves.

It is fitting that one of *Anomalia*'s closing poems begins with self-preservation and ends with the certain jump into a confident future. 'will' starts with death and decomposition, describing the process of rotting as something beautiful, something that preserves:

when I die I will opalise
my bones milky and glinting
blue and green with a tiny
hint of red flitting in and out of sight

It is acceptance of the past, a finishing but not really an ending. In 'will's final lines, I find the future.

I can be found
By archaeologists
I can be gently brushed
I can be displayed
I can be seen
I will be remembered

As a debut collection, *Anomalia* has ballet-leapt confidently onto the centre stage with a surety of step that can only come from knowing it has made its mark.

Jordan Hamel

Jordan Hamel
Everyone Is Everyone Except You
Dead Bird Books, 2021
RRP $30, 65pp

> This is a stick up! What's uglier? Your inside or outside?
> ('Mermaids')

Intro

The front of something is often the first of it we see; the point from which we begin to decode meaning, but the front of something can be slippery. It can be cultivated for purposes of deceit. We have a degree of control over our fronts, they can be salvaged into an appealing shape, one that puts others at ease, unnoticed when mingling with their shapes.

This transmutability has been linguistically internalised; a front can refer to something curated, hiding something else behind or beneath it. Tesla is a front for an investment firm. As a verb, 'fronting' means to show up; it also means to pretend — two interrelated acts.

I'm opening my review of Jordan Hamel's collection with this semantic observation as I believe it is central to the irony of *Everyone Is Everyone Except You* (*EIEEY*). To me, the meaning and brilliance of this book lies in its act — another pretending word.

This collection for me is a tragicomic act of sincere irony, one that seeks to rupture a false dichotomy that posits irony and sincerity as polar aesthetics and principles.

I'm not an academic so it's better to explain by hyperbolising what reading *EIEEY* is like: It is like watching, with tape over your mouth, as a stand-up comedian comes apart after swallowing a grenade. Then, after surviving the explosion, this clown-hero is forced to piece himself together into a shape resembling the comedian he was pre-boom, lest the venue rescind his drink tickets and the audience ask for a refund, leaving him without money for the Uber home. Quite the stage hiccup to overcome already, but this grenade is also the latest advancement in twenty-first-century quantum-metaphysical warfare. It destroys one's body, as grenades tend to, but it also decimates any connotations that body contains, down to its relationship with other bodies and its Netflix password. And from there the analogy devolves further.

The front

The front cover is a framed photograph/painting of a presumably ordinary man, in an ordinary room. His hair is short, neatly parted. Combed to the left, which according to studies makes one appear more competent and masculine. He wears a suit. The right side of his shirt collar overlaps onto a dark blazer. From the sliver of skin we see on his neck, he looks white. His face, however, is missing or gone. In its place is an image of flowers growing on top and beneath one another. No flower more frontward than the rest. A heterogeneous net of nature.

This image of stochastic naturalism is contrasted by the gingham print on the wall behind him, looming with connotations of sexual repression, gender conformity, the nuclear family, and a 1E5 mathematics work book. In relation to the flowers, the gingham is an antithetical demiurge. A dark God of regular angles, manifesting a creation principle of brutal organisation. Homogenous and endlessly predictable in its iterating.

I'm unequipped to determine whether the man's face is obscured by a floral cloth tied around his head or if this construct is erased from memory, a now-absent front replaced entirely by nature's uncoordinated beauty. The flowers are the truth, the soul, the ousia, the id, whatever nomenclature suits. Regardless of terminology, this is what you'd see were this sharply dressed anon to deepthroat Semtex.

Ramblings

EIEEY is a lean 65 pages and is further divided into five parts/acts/chapter/sounders. This is excellent as it integrates an answer for the question: 'How do I read a poetry book?' Additionally, each of the five units seem to cohere and coalesce into their own theme. I'll take the time to detail the first two.

1. Everything, everything will be alright, alright.

This feels taken from dialogue. A rhetorical terminus I can identify from talking to my father, listing the compounding intrinsic and extrinsic reasons as to why I am fucked, and therefore the world is fucked. This title is his reply, preceded by look, or listen, or shut up, 'Everything, (I repeat) everything (whatever the fuck that is), will be alright. Alright.'

This interpretation was spawned by Hamel's depiction of the Kiwi male adolescence. In the space of five short poems, Hamel covers remarkable ground, with an ability to tap simultaneously into aspects that feel both hyper-specific and archetypal.

'Suitcase' details watching a close friend come apart emotionally over a parental divorce, bringing with him the customary box of Double Brown, an unspoken 'If you're gonna be the one crying you bring the piss.'

The repetition of 'For God's sake, don't tell the boys' along with Hamel's recalling of Tony Hawk's *Underground 2* soundtrack hit me with such visceral familiarity I had trouble distinguishing it from my own memory. Another highlight recounts getting booted from Religious Education for placing the sacred SOAD track 'Toxicity' in proximity to the wholly profane 'The Passion of the Christ'.

This poem manages to sublimely navigate and ultimately merge funny with totally fucking miserable. This reminder that absurd bathos and pathos aren't necessarily separate comes in the form of Mel Gibson as 'A proud mum / all motor oil and biceps yelling / You're doing great sweetie! / from behind the camera.'

2. Everyone is supposed to be here except you.

This implies Everyone is here. And so are you. But you're not meant to be. Something about you renders your being here untenable. Unwantable. A cause of irreconcilable friction. You're fucking up the vibe. You have flowers for a face. What a dick. It's a tidy sentence that articulates an implicit tension felt by all who are forced to exist in a Now and figure out what that Now is.

Let's get dialectical, baby.

In art, Now is often discovered by looking into Before, analysing the philosophies that governed its rituals, then honing this analysis into a broad thesis of what Before was. Before is then held in opposition to a speculative antimodel of what Tomorrow will be.

From there, Now's *geist* is synthesised through negotiation between materials provided by thesis and antithesis, meaning Now is chiefly characterised by compromise. 'I guess this is what's going on', as a preferable alternative to 'What the fuck is going on?'

This alternative is preferable as you can construct yourself in relation or reaction to whatever conclusion you come to, regardless of whether it's correct. Deleuze and Guttari would call this an impotent process, and they're correct in a sense, but today feels pretty impotent to me.

In Hamel's narrative we're at the end of the years prescribed to adolescence and are extending further either side of this vector. In our past lies God: the big man is all over this section. He's our thesis and he comes out swinging in 'if you read this backwards blood becomes wine'. The poem is loaded with symmetries between biblical tradition and modern capitalism: 'When I'm ready to bear fruit / it will be less . . . transubstantiation / more . . . Initial Public Offering.'

Later in the chapter we arrive at our antithesis, The Camera. It is a deliberately fraught antithesis as it is loaded with and symbolic of continuity, representing the past and the future. A democratised technology used to document Now's becoming of Before, and a deeply commodifying agent. It is our current cultural direction — that tool making this possible.

The camera is also a prelapsarian symbol. When lamenting the alienating social landscape of the twenty-first century, as politically atomised individuals, the endemic death-zone many remark upon is Hollywood. What happened to the stars? The Glitz? Everything seemed so possible. How did we fuck it up so bad? Yesterday saw Tomorrow as loaded with potential, too bad we live in Now.

In this chapter we see Hamel caught between God and the camera, struggling to synthesise and exist Now. My fave poem of this chapter is '*in media res*', which translates roughly to 'in the midst of things'. This analysis is overwrought and nearly all BS, so I'm going to mash a quote from '*in media res*' into a quote from the poem that follows '*To be continued*', and hope that illustrates whatever my point is:

> I'm terrified of the credits,
> Never knowing if they're opening
> Or closing
>
> But the camera still lingers not letting me
> Dissolve into something else

I'll finish now.

The pain of the modern day, particularly for Western white men with middle-class backgrounds, is a meandering pain. A 'call Mum' pain. It's not having your leg severed by a drone strike. It's ennui, which I don't mean dismissively; I feel it like a fucking knife.

Ennui is a bored pain, an elsewhere pain that comes from wondering who you are and where your place is, only to find there is no place and you're not really . . .

> God is a comedian playing to an audience that is too afraid to laugh.
> — Voltaire.

Liam Hinton

essa may ranapiri

essa may ranapiri
Echidna
Te Herenga Waka University Press, 2022
RRP $25, 96pp

Echidna
or
The Many Adventures of
Hinenakahirua as She Tries to Find
Her Place in a Colonised World
included throughout is the story of Maui-Potiki & Prometheus

A light to burn all the empires, so bright the sun is ashamed to rise and be.
(Milton, 'Paradise Lost')

Intro & Dramatis Personae | He Tangata

What begins to be by spreading?

The number seven bears significance within most theologies of the world, some of which are known without ever encountering physical or digital scripture: seven days of creation, seven capital vices, etc.

I plumbed my shallow depths for every instance I could recall, because *Echidna* is divided into seven sections and I wanted to identify a significance. essa may ranapiri is a complex and layered artist, whose work has me searching for meaning in every alcove (I probably missed a cryptographic cipher hidden in the publication details). *Echidna* deals closely with Māori mythology; I wanted to recall an instance of seven therein, but was unable to do so due to unfamiliarity. Matariki was my first thought, but it appears there are nine stars and this is another thing I was wrong about, and Googling has left me less sure than I was to begin with.

I came across a Wikipedia entry for sevens within religion and myth, which dedicates most of its page space on this topic to the widest practised religions. It also details occurrences of seven within Mithraism, Gnosticism, Baltic myth, Mesopotamian myth, and Galician folklore. It details the fingers, feet and pupils of Cú Chulainn. It also features the seven super-universes in the cosmology of Urantia; I know nothing about this save for it's less than 100 years old (which I *thiiiink* makes it a cult?).

I thought maybe seven simply wasn't an important number in Māori mythology, however I did come across the Seven Whales of Ngāi Tahu Matawhaiti. Maybe Wikipedia has a blindspot for Māori culture: the page on the number three in myths also omits the three kete of knowledge.

I turned back to the contents page to see whether there were any more discoveries that might be made. In addition to remixing the Māori and Christian mythological canons, Grecian mythology is present in *Echidna*. I knew many of these figures — it's difficult not to, given their prevalence within modern pop culture.

Two big things hit me and I hadn't even made it to the first poem.

1. I don't live in Greece, I live here, and know fuck all about here.
2. How many people's stories are left out of the most commonly accessed centres of knowledge.

In addition to having a one-word title, *Echidna* also features a long-ass subtitle, *The Many Adventures of Hinenakahirua as She Tries to Find Her Place in a Colonised World*. In reading this collection, I found much of the poems' place-finding came in the forms of struggle and loss. To exist shouldn't be something one has to fight for, but to quote 'She viper-with Tales Outstretched', Echidna 'chooses violence cos what choice does she really have?'

Every review of *Echidna* will discuss the Dramatis Personae | He

Tangata (DP | HT), which should be reason to avoid doing so, but I cannot fucking help myself. This thing ROCKS so hard it's poetry unto itself. It features an ensemble cast of figures from myth, pop culture, our shitty material plain and the radiant pleroma that is ranapiri's batshit brain.

When introducing Echidna herself, DP | HT is reverent and playful: 'Mother of Monsters & messy takatapui wahine.'

When introducing Musk, it is taunting: 'Sent a car to space as a show of power.'

When introducing Bezos, it is implicitly threatening: 'When not if.'

When introducing Narcissus, it tests your pun tolerance: 'A person with great interest in reflection.'

When introducing Zoa, it is gorgeously anarchic, charged with potentiality and personality: 'Two-spirit Oji-Cree, also a cyborg with a soul of glitter.'

The section can be read as a democratising agent, placing figures known, unknown and unknowable in proximity. Presuming or enforcing a lack of familiarity with them all. It's also dictatorial.

If *Echidna* says Typhon is 'a good lay', this is true.

If Echidna says The Spider is 'the coolest bish around', this is not an opinion. Believe that shit.

On Echidna (the character not the book . . . sort of)

What hot summer is a snake doing in New Zealand?

If Echidna shoved me against the wall of a dark alley, pressed a fang/quill/fingernail to my neck, and commanded me to summarise them in one word, I would diplomatically respond, 'busy'. (I don't think men can get away calling her 'messy' as ranapiri can.)

Echidna is a lot, maybe everything. As the Mother of Monsters maybe they are everything *else*. There are many tendrils to Echidna and they are hard to pin down. She is a deliberate contradiction: their life begins by ending, and ends by beginning. They are child and mother, impulsive and pensive, violent and gentle, barbed and longing for touch. Perhaps for Echidna to survive in this world we've built around her/them, she/they has to be a lot of different things.

It is difficult to even understand the dimensions of Echidna's physical form, a difficulty Echidna often shares with the reader. It would be easy for this elusive and mutagenic quality to make Echidna unrelatable, but for everything that rendered Echidna stranger to me, there was something else that made her feel familiar.

Echidna dresses in hand-me-down clothes and plays atop the hydrangeas. Their dad's got a bit of an 'old testament rage', the way many fathers have. Her relatability and self-form confusion is front and centre in 'Echidna Goes Through Her Emo Phase' — likely a hit single from this concept album. Like many teenagers, Echidna is in her room. Alone with books, CDs, her Gerard Way poster and her body.

It's an incredible poem; it bounces with movement and humour, but it's also intimate, deeply private and personal. Echidna is writing out lyrics to an AFI album (?), thumb holes chewed in her sleeves. The poem again demonstrates this collection's magical ability to amalgamate and lateralise theological, mythological, linguistic and literary canons (it is fitting that a text featuring Echidna screaming *ACABACABACAB* at a karaoke bar is fixed on the abolition of such hierarchies).

essa may ranapiri has such total control and understanding of Echidna as a character, the poem feels as if it were somehow written by her. Echidna's teenage sadness is beautiful and urgent and doesn't factor time to evaluate whether Milton is a bigger deal than My Chem. To Echidna, at this stage in their evolution, it's all new stimulus, it's all so real, it all matters so fucking much.

I can't detail Echidna's entire journey here, you'll have to buy the book, but every one of the numerous poems that centre their story is equally precise in its articulation. Echidna is a lot and all of it is compelling, spiritual, true and grounded.

> She wraps cliches around herself to get dry / the mirror fogged over /
> hides a reflection she doesn't see herself in.
> ('Echinda Goes Through Her Emo Phase')

PS: Another highlight is 'Echidna Tries Her Best to Console Herculine'. I sincerely implore you give it a read. The final line had me in tears. Rest in power.

On Māui-Pōtiki and Prometheus

its a small text in the late hours

Māui-Pōtiki & Prometheus belongs to the genre of slash fic, fan fic that focuses on romantic or sexual relationships between fictional characters of the same sex.

At first glance, slash-fic is kind of absurd. It's a popular artform amongst Tumblr users and often features figures from texts these users gravitate towards. But much of its impetus comes from how often these texts engage in queerbaiting; teasing the presence of a queer dimension without exploring or depicting anything explicitly queer. Part of what might make slash-fic conceptually 'cringe' is the sincerity of its longing, both of author and character. Sincerity makes lots of people uncomfortable, but it can also make for very good and honest art.

Māui and Prometheus's story was my favourite section of *Echidna.* It is moving, erotic and heart-wrenching. It is also an incredible demonstration of slash-fic's potential. It certainly made me reconsider the subtly malicious motivations I might've had for dismissing it. Māui and Prometheus's love broke my little heart. It's a twenty-first-century romantic tragedy of mythic proportions that I'll likely remember forever. I think it'll be studied. I think it'll be emulated. I could even envision it being adapted on screen or stage. That's the kind of book this is.

> he's been here before waiting for a boulder to roll back from a black hole
> where something should be.
> ('Prometheus at the Crucifixion')

Outro

Echidna is brilliant. I'm not the first one to say this. I won't be the last. It's genius all the way down. It's personal and political (as if these things were ever separate), and has every potential to thrust neglected stories into the wider culture that have long belonged there.

It is completely ranapiri and a worthy artistic representation of their person in the world, but most of all this book is an incredible act of generosity, and will mean so much to so many. It's an important book. I hope it is everywhere. I hope teenagers read through it. I hope everyone reads it, and I hope they click all the hyperlinks books will one day possess (Bezos's will be underlined in red). And on the Wiki entry for the symbolism of seven, I hope we find documented the seven chapters of Hinenakahirua, the mythological stowaway and messy takatāpui wahine who made Aotearoa their imperfect home in a colonised world.

> Over the burial she holds / the / clay from her whenua plays some / impotent notes into it and / feels free
> ('Hinenakahirua Repairs Something That Needs Repairing')

Mark Houlahan

Anna Jackson

Anna Jackson
Actions & Travels
Auckland University Press, 2022
RRP $35, 300pp

When this book was first in AUP's listing of things soon-to-be-published, I instantly put an advance order in to my local bookstore and then devoured it as soon as it came to hand. It did not disappoint. Anyone reading *Poetry Aotearoa* will be charmed, informed and delighted by this book. I've never been in Anna Jackson's poetry classroom but the sense you get here is that she must be a stellar teacher of poetry.

The setup is easily explained. In 10 chapters Jackson takes us through 10 ratios or contexts for grasping 'how poetry works', and in each chapter she works through details of several poems to illustrate the point. This is how poetry works in granular detail. In all, we get Jackson's view of a hundred poems ranging from highly canonical poets like the Roman Catullus through to contemporary American poets and a good sampling of very fresh work by poets of Aotearoa New Zealand. Jackson excludes herself from this selection of poems to discuss, but her own poetic practice is, in a sense, just out of sight. Most of the poems are quoted in full, and can all be found on her website at www.annajackson.nz/actions-and-travels.html.

Modestly, Jackson claims that this is not a scholar's book, and it's not festooned with footnotes, so that if you want to quickly remind yourself, for example, what tetrameter is, you can quickly look elsewhere. I took this as a modern version of a modesty topos, as the book is nevertheless deeply learned and digests several decades of reading and writing poetry (Jackson sees these as intertwined actions). The great skill here is in representing that learning so deftly and lightly, with such assurance and grace. Jackson's father is a formidable scholar of English Renaissance poetry (and a great teacher himself). I don't know whether scansion was required at the family breakfast table. If so, that has really paid off.

The chapters here aren't designed to give a comprehensive view of poetry in general (an impossible labour in a single book). Rather each lights on a different aspect of poetry that Jackson finds engaging. The aspects are allowed to jostle with each other and contradict. For example, Chapter 3 focuses on 'Concision, composition & the image', and leads us through Pound's 'In a Station of the Metro' and William Carlos Williams' 'Red Wheelbarrow', still small miracles of photographic insight on the page. And yet fetishising these small, jewel-like moments, Jackson shows, is not all there is to poetry.

So we turn to Chapter 4, for the opposite energy, 'Sprawl', a nicely ironic one-word title. Here we find Whitman and Ginsberg with their spilling, messily epic styles, busting out beyond the 10 syllables of pentameter, trying somehow to cram all of the America they knew onto the page. It's democratic, inclusive, crossing the line between making poetry and making a journal or writing a letter. We might think of that kind of writing as being 'prose', but, as Jackson suggests, in the age of twitter poems and poems made global through YouTube anything goes, as Gershwin so joyously put it in the modernist 1920s.

Jackson relishes poetry of the 'now', and is generous here in drawing out the emerging energy of a new generation of Aotearoa poets: Hera Lindsay Bird, Tayi Tibble, essa may ranapiri among them. These poets have concerns not directly addressed in traditional poetry, as they grapple with climate change and unfolding gender diversity and the aftershocks of colonisation. Sometimes, Jackson suggests, such poets can seem dismissive of the tradition, as in Bird's notorious 'Keats is dead, so fuck me from behind'. Yet in her selections of poems for each chapter, Jackson blends contemporary poets with those from other centuries. New poets, she shows, are often reworking tropes and forms from other times and places.

If you prefer poets who use fixed forms, she can show you ways to think about new poets who can seem baffling. If you think the old is boring she lights up magic places in all kinds of poems from Shakespeare to Marvell and Catullus. You could think of the book as an imaginary museum of poetry Jackson has curated. In each room or chapter, generations of poetic voices jostle and converse with each other.

In another act of modesty Jackson does not use examples from her own substantial body of poems. Yet, as so often when working poets use their critical voice, she is offering up clues to her own poetic, even while being so resourceful in helping us think through some poetry fundamentals. So Jackson wields small details in poems superbly, but she also uses the sprawl effect at times. Sometimes she uses a persona, and at others she makes a poem-diary taken right from her life. She discusses Karl Stead, among others, in dialogue with Catullus (this section is rivetingly well informed).

Jackson has two excellent volumes in the same vein, *Catullus for Children* and *I, Clodia*. The book opens with Keats's great fragment, 'This living hand', which Jackson codes as an image of the power of the poem to reach out across centuries and claim us, part of what in her final chapter she describes as the realm of 'Poetry & the afterlife'. In this frame, all poetry becomes a form of elegy and epitaph. For this effect in practice, see Jackson's sprawling mini-epic *Dear Tombs, Dear Horizon*, where elegy, epitaph, ghosting and travel writing all combine luminously.

Jackson has made a really good book, and AUP has produced a very handsome volume, so easy to dip in and out of. The index is super helpful. Soon enough you'll find your own copy peppered with Post-its, as mine is now, marking poems and Jacksonian observations that you'll want to come back to and cite: 'Jackson says'.

Elizabeth Kirkby-McLeod

Jennifer Compton

Jennifer Compton
the moment, taken
Recent Work Press, 2021
RRP $24.99, 80pp

This is the eleventh collection from Jennifer Compton (a New Zealand-born poet known and awarded both here and in her adopted home of Australia). It is organised into two sections, Compton noting that in the first she 'eschews capital letters . . . with an egalitarian spirit', while in the second, she returns to the 'burden of formal written language' (with the second half stronger for that return) (if you have been irritated by this paragraph so far then these might not be the poems for you — they are progressively inhabited by bracketed text (even a cat takes part, leaving brackets within brackets)).

Inhabited. That's a good word to describe this collection. In the poem 'once', creatures inhabit the speaker's raincoat sleeve, her shoes, even her face, while creatures return to occupy her body again in grotesque form in the poem 'We All Go Together'. The poems are infused by an awareness of who else, and what else, inhabits Compton's world — whether living, dead, famous or unknown.

In 'in the park, a family' Compton stacks up words in short lines as she observes a family stacked up, lying and sitting atop one another. On the next page an 'old guy fell dead' in the doorstop of a post office in 'the post office, the postmaster'. In 'the view from below', the poem's speaker walks through a suburb presenting to us people both present and remembered: 'the Greek olds', 'the grandson next door', 'women screaming', cumulating in 'a gangling, solitary man' who, unlike the poet, fails to notice the world around him:

loped athwart me, on his own path
not a nod in my direction

as if he didn't notice me
(he didn't even notice me)
tipping his cheap treat

from a sleek, rippable bag
into his mouth

into his appetite

What did you think of that 'athwart'? How about 'alarum' found in the poem 'Timeshare in Coolangata'? These words pop out at me, precisely because they are words that don't inhabit the world Compton is attempting to show us, the world she is inhabiting. There is so much to like in Compton's poems, there are many people to meet, but also many distractions — why the brackets? Why the arcane language pops? What is it about capital letters that makes them elitist?

Put aside these questions and there is pleasure to be had in the poems, especially where Compton engages with the work of other female artists in a series of poems near the beginning of the second section. Writer Janet Frame, painter Grace Cossington Smith and photographer Olive Cotton all have work examined by the poet. She enriches them with her own imaginings while noting, 'Nothing I am imagining is as true as it was true' ('Take').

Maggie Rainey-Smith

Maggie Rainey-Smith
Formica
The Cuba Press, 2022
RRP $25, 86pp

In *Formica*, Maggie Rainey-Smith captures Aotearoa New Zealand as it lurched through decades of change, from post-Second World War to today. These changes are mirrored in the poet herself and through her family situation, then taken and set like scratches in a Formica tabletop in taut, specific descriptions: 'he proposed on the ghost / train and she screamed / as the skeletons rattled' ('Love in the fifties'); 'kindling in / a coal bucket' ('After the war'); 'he's angry at the over- / ripe sun' ('Siem Reap').

Rainey-Smith takes us through changing times in a changing country, by catching a thought or event from one poem and moving it on to the next; the collection is not narrative, but the poems are connected. 'Autumn and Anzac' finds a family rising to a day full of sorrow and drunkenness with their father, a survivor of the war, 'a fatherless lad, POW, returned'. It is followed by 'Seventy years on', where history is being reviewed, the costs of war counted, the boys and men lost once to war, twice to time, and now to revision.

This moving through time and thought can happen within one poem. At the beginning of 'That Summer', two girls are young, fresh and freckled, the speaker remembering a time before marriage, a time before a brother takes his own life. By the poem's end, these girls have become grandmothers, 'with river stones and / gravel in our hearts'.

Rainey-Smith charts these changes mostly with sympathy and a desire to 'still want to play / to flaunt in twilight' ('Menopause') — which makes the odd time she stereotypes women a jarring experience. In 'Swiss Ball' and 'Jogging', the poet is older, judging and dismissive of the young women around her, not allowing them the complex inner life we have seen the poet enjoy:

I'm relieved I'm not a tight bright
Bum in fluro who trades sex for
Income or sex for a South Pacific bure
— I can earn my own holidays, thanks

An odd lack of compassion in an otherwise insightful collection.

Dinah Hawken

Dinah Hawken
Sea-light
Te Herenga Waka University Press, 2021
RRP $25, 60pp

This, Dinah Hawken's ninth collection, has a tidal quality — the poems change and alter in perspective, from crystalline moments of detail and stillness to wide-open vistas filled with emotion. There are scenes Hawken observes from some distance, and others that she climbs inside.

In the middle of a still life aching with danger and love, this blink-of-an-eye snapshot finds peacefulness: 'The book / has been lifted up // absorbed // and placed carefully down.' In other places, she turns her gaze on herself, the one person for whom her patience sometimes falters — 'On the defensive', as she once sums herself up — and archly instructs herself in a poem titled 'Self-talk of a stern nature' to 'Try reclamation. Be like the moon / and stand around shamelessly / in borrowed light'.

The sea, the other powerful voice in these poems, speaks of tranquillity and of trouble. At times it is a force of relentless approach ('The sea is coming straight for us / line after line like an old-fashioned army'); at other times it corresponds with the body and the land, not at all as if it could be tamed, but perhaps the opposite:

> The sea is coming in friendship
> with deep breathing and
> an offering of small shells.

I love you like this, Pacific,
when you come bearing your name . . .
('The sea')

Strands of story form at their own pace as the collection progresses. The grief that attends her sister's death has its own eddying pull, and it returns to tell pieces of the stories that make up a relationship not easily ended:

I used to think 'pass away'
was a euphemism,
a kind of cowering,
but since my sister died
I believe in pass
and I believe in away
('You never know')

The poems that carry this narrative are heartbreaking and viscerally moving. They leave gaps that cannot be filled, and sketch over details that might or might not reveal more of a beloved one.

I held the urn against me
as if my sister was unborn
and walked with her
on the closed-in verandah
of her last wordly home . . .

I turned into a kuia
and filled the house
with the echo
and groundswell of grief.
('A small woman returning in a blue urn')

Much here is political, in several shades of what that might mean; much, also, is focused on the interplay of the natural landscape and the landscape of the body. Hawken writes of her own breast cancer and the surgery that shaped her body's sense of age — her scar anchoring time's passing across her chest. Then she turns to the scarred soil and the waterways groaning under the pressures of production: 'Most fisherman don't want to collapse / the fish stocks. Not quickly anyway.'

With her physiotherapist's eye, her trained skill of listening, Hawken notices intently — but, often, refrains from intervention. Her touch is delicate and subtle, without force. Though she opens with the words of Rebecca Solnit, calling for a portrayal of such possibility 'that people wander out of their bunkers, / put down their weapons and come over', these poems are not purposeful or pushy; they have a diffident self-possession that lets them invite reflection.

> Mystery lives round the edges
> of things and although the midwife
> has two hands, the dragonfly two eyes
>
> and there are two incredible hemispheres,
> mystery comes in the odd numbers
> with no intention to be clear.
> ('Haze')

Hawken's career in letters has been long, and as she reflects, perhaps, on the lifetime of words, her voice is restful and generous: 'Self is a soft word, like loft and lift // it is best seen in a soft light.'

Anne Kennedy

Anne Kennedy
The Sea Walks into a Wall
Auckland University Press, 2021
RRP $24.99, 92pp

In this substantial collection, the world is sharply observed and inspected upside down. The poet approaches matters with an intensity, a curiosity, that colours them vividly; her voice is unmistakeable and unselfconscious. Words roll around on her tongue. They don't always make good sense, unless that's exactly what they're doing.

Half a lifetime ago, I was Anne Kennedy's student. At the front of an English literature classroom she would notice and point to the world's large and small injustices — not the loudest of her colleagues but one who paid attention to things inside and outside of her own experience.

> All winter the rain blubs on the shoulders of Ihumātao.
> The main drag splutters under people's gumboots.
> ('Two waters')

It's impossible to read these poems and not be moved, bodily squirmed by the delicious tastes and textures she finds in daily happenings. This, for example, from a three-part cycle called 'Lights On in the Garden', where she picks, magpie-like, through the workings of the institute where she taught creative writing, its upper management removed 'geographically, culturally, squeamishly' from their students and staff:

> The very reverend executive team all live as far from the polytechnic
> as it is possible to live
> while still being technically domiciled in the supercity because
> unfortunately

the polytech is situated
in a part of town that is quite problematic for a modern major executive.
It might look hip,
with its markets, food, music, dance, its elders sitting talking
in the shopping centre
at lunch time, but they are working people, they are brown and scary,
plus there are a lot of them.

Depressing, perhaps, but lifted by the love that Kennedy holds for all ridiculous beings, all times and people and places and predicaments; she finds moments to love in discomfort and restriction ('I've had amazing times / camping / on planes. // My pillow my blanket my / dinner / on a plane') and in commitment and tedium ('For several months you hold the car door open for toddlers. / Weeks watching the progress of mercury in a thermometer. / Several years the pages of critical theory kept you from death'). That's not to suggest that her words aren't often pointy, but they explore more than they pin down.

These poems span expanses of time and place — the sounds of Hawai'i are here, Mrs Dalloway's London, the workshops of Iowa and the titular seawall at Island Bay. Kennedy is far from disoriented, just breathlessly dubious about some of the certainties on offer:

I thought it was that aria ('Remember me')
but it was the washing machine on spin.

I thought it was the bells ringing out
from St Joseph's the Mrkusich church.

It was dial up-knocking on the door
to the internet . . .
('The Book of Changes')

In the deceptive way of all really good teachers, Kennedy has organised these pieces as if scattered. Subtle, accessible, perfectly up-to-date, they are the works of a master of her craft, and a glorious introduction to her voice. This collection is a treasure — in among the tinfoil, not a jewel out of place.

Abigail Marshall

Rachel O'Neill

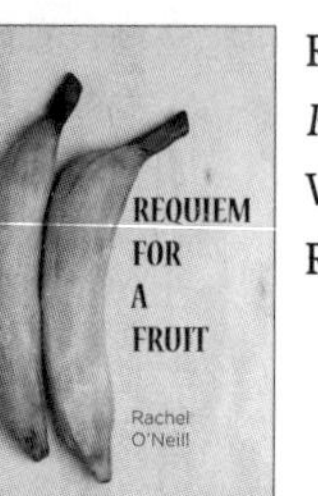

Rachel O'Neill
Requiem for a Fruit
We Are Babies, 2021
RRP $25, 58pp

I stepped inside *Requiem for a Fruit* and was, on entry, delightfully lost. Rachel O'Neill's prose-poetry collection shimmers with detail. It's full of moments from everyday life that have been distorted with wild imagination. Sometimes reading it feels like leafing through a natural history book — one that has been cut up and découpaged together again. The poems slip up onto the page:

> I begin installation tentatively at first — mothers and fathers, sisters, mistresses and boys. My confidence grows and I'm off — winged creatures, lowly amphibians, cloths stained with tincture, detached heads of wheat
> ('The subterranean hotel')

From this vantage point on the outskirts of reality, O'Neill chooses to show readers a heavy world. Everyday troubles morph into surrealist jokes, and feelings grow up to be carnivorous beasts. In 'a reason for everything' O'Neill's deep struggle with the meaning of life spins into a pun. Unexpected turns such as these force us to take another look at the lives we live.

For this poet, what can be understood about life seems kind of slippery. They're constantly peering at the undersides of existence. They question accepted explanations and point out humour where other poets might write angst-filled sonnets. That's not to say that anxiety is dismissed; rather, it's sort of loved into another existence. 'Whatever that means', a little half-page poem, addresses the issues of death and discrimination. O'Neill upsets the expected tone of such a piece by exploring how a ghost might feel about the bureaucracy and bigotry of the afterlife.

Many of the poems take this step into mysterious absurdity at one point or another. O'Neill struggles with many questions, but they will not give us the pleasure of a simple answer. It would not be beautiful enough. In 'Look again' they place readers at a window and demand they take a new approach to looking out at the scene below:

> Look again at the long cracks. Why are the two men hammering that red-hot shape? What is the third man, on the left, doing? Which person is not showing agreement with these ideas? Do these belong in a Victorian drawing room? How does this nest compare with other nests that you have seen? Prick it with a needle. Were they poisoned? Why are there so many veins underneath? Compare it to the 21st Century. What is left?

What's left after reading many of the collection's poems are impressions, feelings and images. The crystal-clear details within plot-shattered poems hold our attention to the page. The words are lush, dripping with fleshy uncertainty. They confuse and delight. I fell in love with the sonic quality in descriptions of a 'mulched tundra' and leaves that 'withered and sizzled and ricocheted and cramped like an exploding arboretum of dehydrated guts'. They act as the fruit of a philosophical forest, evidence of meanings hidden under their surreal humour. Here, the prose-poem format helps to keep things in order by pairing the images with simple speech patterns. Each poem is written as if O'Neill is in the room, narrating wild stories over a cup of tea. They may speak in riddles, but they speak them in plain language.

It's clear, despite the strangeness of the poems, that O'Neill still cares about what's happening in real life. This is seen in their poems on gender identity. They reveal a desire to find a place of peace; finding none, they turn to creativity. 'The fantasy is expressing what a subtext that has grown merciless looks like', they write. O'Neill hides behind this fantasy shield to survive an environment that has not always accepted them. Whether they are concerned with their existential suffering or their overload of housework, O'Neill constantly questions whether anything is worth facing in bare reality:

> 'If I could look again, I would,' is the usual reply from those who dare to peek at the most hellish painting in the world.
> ('The supernatural frame')

And so, O'Neill struggles on to see the world up close, never trying to explain experiences through pure reason. They subvert story tropes, add imaginative extensions to overheard dialogue and set common frustrations in alien worlds. In doing so, they create an atmosphere that allows them to breathe.

The collection ends with 'Common Greetings'. It considers returning to a singular way of existing in the world, but by the end of the book we know that's not going to happen:

> I practise writing my name until it appears to belong to someone strange who cuts corners and stretches elastic and purrs in the middle of a sentence . . . I keep track of all the extinct names as I'm not above repeating myself . . . my life in the English language isn't over . . . So, that's me, Goodbye Hello.

When I finished *Requiem for a Fruit*, I felt that its way of revealing and reinventing the world around us had rubbed off on me. Lines keep coming back to me, even though I've placed the book, tidy and contained, on a shelf. It has left some 'winged creatures, lowly amphibians' lurking in the back of my mind.

Abigail Marshall

Nicole Titihuia Hawkins

Nicole Titihuia Hawkins
Whai
We Are Babies, 2021
RRP $25, 90pp

Nicole Titihuia Hawkins, an Aotearoa poet, teacher and proud aunty, steps onto the page mid-drama with her debut poetry collection. *Whai* begins:

> I grew up in hand-cut knickers
> stitched on Mum's tino taonga.

Hawkins goes on to trace the threads of her parents' lives from her early years until after their relationship's complex rupture. She watches two separations occurring: one between her father and mother and one between her and her heritage. Throughout the collection, Hawkins wrestles with how to deal with this experience. She wants to know where she has come from, and how she can get back what has been lost. She writes to her mother:

> On the day of my birth
> you gave me a diluted tipuna name
> resurrected it postpartum
> perhaps the traces of my Māori blood lingered
> ('On the day of my birth')

Whai won the Jessie Mackay Prize for the best first book of poetry at the Ockham New Zealand Book Awards in 2022. It's easy to see why. It is bold, polished and unflinchingly honest. There are not many times when a debut reads so effortlessly or packs such an emotional punch. Reading it takes you on a compact journey through the past, present and future. At times I was thrilled as I absorbed it, curled up in safety on the couch. Sometimes I felt like a guest, getting to pull back the curtain on someone's life and look in. It is a dynamic series on identity; a poet reminding herself of what is hers:

> it's not from not knowing the kupu
> I can tell you where I'm from
> but I still search
> pulling back the pale skin
> from my wrists
> so I can read the
> blue green map of Mokaka awa
> ('Carrying blood back to my heart')

Within Hawkins' search, there is a deep sense of loss. She knows that her efforts are only needed because of colonial and misogynistic destruction. She addresses its impact on her life, her whānau and her work with students and academics.

Despite the complex subject matter, the poems never feel like history lessons or a textbook. When Hawkins has a point to make, she shows it through personal stories. Misogyny is found in the voice of a boy who wants a 'less-lippy' woman for a wife. Racism appears in organisations that refuse to say the word.

She recalls everything from revealing car rides with students to clueless comments from ex-boyfriends. These snippets of reality lift the poems off the page. Some bring quiet devastation, others jump up wry and witty. They fit together to paint a picture, but there are no broad brushstrokes here; each character is revealed in unique detail. This is seen powerfully in 'Rua tekau mā waru', where examples of feminine shame and stigma are shown in individuals' lives, ingrown like hairs. Even in this struggle, humour peeks through:

I complain about the pain,
Order two different types of fries.
At the end of the first basket she says she feels
Herself being pulled into my orbit
Stop Bluetoothing me.

This dedication to character lends itself to language choices that feel natural — as if the poet's world has been submerged below water and the necessary words and stanza patterns have floated to the top. Even tightly structured poems, such as the spherical 'Kina eyes', flow easily within their form. Hawkins' mastery of language makes it disappear from view, leaving unique voices sounding from the age. Dialogue fits comfortably into the lines. Spirited text messages appear throughout. Couples argue. Racist structures exist behind the words of 'An exchange: three emails'. Student–teacher conversations shine in 'Kaiako Dialogues'. A niece at the marae questions Hawkins:

Why aren't we getting up   Aunty?
Why don't we know the words   Aunty?
('Matariki')

The role and power of language are paramount throughout the book. English and te reo Māori interact continuously, a reflection of colonised Aotearoa. Despite a great deal of pressure, te reo refuses to be smoked out. Instead, it lives in the very structure of the book, which is laid out like a kapa haka weave.

Hawkins is not afraid to point out the resistance to her language. Having led readers to grow attached to her humorous characters, she can just as easily break hearts by showing the strained side of their statements. Things get serious, the importance of each throwaway comment adds up throughout the poems; words and silences are the very substance of Hawkins' experience of interacting with others. In 'How to prepare for isolation', she considers the possibility of her life without someone who can share words with her in the way that she needs:

Read that if you die
your fevered body
will go straight to the urupā
no one will be there to karanga
when they lower you steaming
into Papa's embrace
no one will be there to wail for you

At the end of *Whai*, I was left with a question: Who will karanga for us in the future? There is a clear challenge for connection, justice and healing implicit in Hawkins' work. I often sensed loss in the blank spaces, but I also felt the warmth of possibility in the sprawl of its verses. There are times when *Whai* reads as a woven lifeline. There are times when the words reach around — an answer to their own call.

Hana Pera Aoake

Hana Pera Aoake
A Bathful of Kawakawa and Hot Water
Compound Press, 2021
RRP $25–$35, 94pp

'Perhaps we should've stayed. Sometimes the longing might kill you. Other times it might just be the exhaustion', writes Hana Pera Aoake in their stunning and intimate collection *A Bathful of Kawakawa and Hot Water*. It is a beautiful collection about resilience, hope, family and everything in between, and from the very first sentence, I knew this book would take me for one hell of a ride — one I wasn't entirely prepared for.

The book, beautifully printed and hand bound by Chris Holloway at Compound Press, starts from . . . the very beginning. When Aoake's tūpuna sailed across the ocean towards Aotearoa, following the safe path of Pane-iraira, they settled on this whenua — crowned on Ihumātao intense and breath-taking recollection of Aoake's life — from the womb to the shores of Lisboa, Portugal, and back again.

It's through Aoake's birth that we're born, too, that we begin a connection with our own ancestors and homeland; we begin to feel an intense connection with our past selves. And as soon as our feet connect with the earth, we are taken on a journey, through untouched terrain, exposed to a new level of anger and frustration, to beauty and hope and to the intimate mind of the author. Stopping to take a breath is not an option. What strikes me the most about this collection is how quickly I go from a fuelled ball of hot rage into fits of laughter. Aoake's ability to evoke such an intense array of emotions is awe inspiring.

This story is told through sections: each part unique and bold, yet somehow cohesive and brilliantly strung together. The sequence moves and sways the reader from one world to another. Part 1, my favourite section, reads like a long and angry Twitter rant. All caps. Like a fiery poem. Like a waiata.

From Aotearoa we are taken to the streets of Portugal. From birth to death. From justified rage to justified grief. Aoake's imagery and unique voice are a powerful combination. Their words are compelling. Intense. Their voice leaves nowhere for the reader to hide. It's a reckoning with every turning page. Through both a retelling of their own experiences and pieces of prose poetry, the reader becomes immersed in everything that is Aoake's. Their voice. Their writing. It is as poignant as it is heartbreaking.

> I wonder if a soul is like a wairua, but that seems too limited. I imagine a wairua with the power of a thousand hearts beating together simultaneously in the air, the soil, and in the living and non-living matter that encompasses everything.
> ('the only way out is through')

As a person of colour (particularly as a Black Hijabi woman) this book feels to me as if someone has rudely entered the dark corners of my brain and pulled out the ugly things I have kept hidden. It feels as if someone has flicked through the pages of my own life and taken picture after picture, held a mirror up to the things I cannot bear to look at. Every page is a painful inhale. Every word is a painful exhale.

I remember it all, like that moment when I was 10, desperately scrubbing the skin of my forearms in the bathroom sink after school because my tiny body could no longer carry the weight of being so different. I was heaving under the pressure. In *A Bathful of Kawakawa and Hot Water* that 10-year-old girl has been ripped out of the grooves of my brain, placed right in front of me, and I stare at her. Eyelids threatening to burst.

Aoake has bathed the pain in a bright white light. Forced me to reckon with a part of myself I had thought was long forgotten. They have forced me to sit with the uncomfortable. They have allowed me to feel angry. And as each emotion moves through me, I feel deeply healed.

> I'm an urban Maaori, constantly switching, hiding and being adaptable.
> My skin tone fluctuates, but it's always a point of tension and pain.
> ('the only way out is through')

A Bathful of Kawakawa and Hot Water has made me, daughter of Somali refugees, living nestled in the Wellington hills, feel seen and heard. Not only am I completely disjointed and torn apart at the seams by every page but I am also slowly pieced back together by the end. And every word they've written feels like a silent promise. To my past self. To 10-year-old me. And to every reader that immerses themselves in Aoake's words.

Janet Charman

Janet Charman
The Pistils
Otago University Press, 2022
RRP $25, 84pp

Janet Charman's poetry is no wallflower, despite the insistence of a diminutive pronominal 'i'. The poems in her ninth collection, *The Pistils*, shrug off their petals and storm the pages with the politic and the personal, with cutting wit and the blunter edges of the domestic scape, hazed with memories of bach gardens and picnic sets. The 'i' moves between poems, holding its own in a world in which literary significance is determined by men, but in which women are defiant.

There are moments of softness, a 'frock summer', river bathing, scenes that delight in having a mother, or in being a mother, pantomimes and pyjamas. But there is a shadow to the sun-lit yards, a revelation that the gardens are temporary, that the domestic is a place of severity, of 'dark internal kitchen(s)', that memory is a balding thing punctuated by the shock of adult happenings — the *Wahine* disaster, cultural injustices, the felling of trees, a conscience of 'boys and their nooses', the grievances of sex.

Charman's world summons the quaint metrics of youth: 'about / from here to the dairy', but her adult life is quantified by the yardsticks of a temporality that is damning:

> sometime
> the other dead
> you or i
> will wake up in this bed
> ('12. Labour Day')

Adulthood figures in an absence — a loss of mothers, spouses, aunts. The garden that 'was meant to last / forever' with 'the magnolia in leaf / all the flowers over' devolves into 'our new one / bought off the plan'. The ancient mattresses are cast out, the egg-yolk blankets repurposed, a mother is lost, 'the birds fly away', the partner's gaze that had 'surveilled the microwave window' in a ritual of Bircher and porridge is gone. This is poetry as elegy in the very best sense — a mourning of the delicate ceremonies of the everyday.

The Pistils jabs its elbow into the patriarchy, in a shock of poems where plant morphology and women's sexuality come together, full-frontal and bold. Georgia O'Keefe loiters in these poems of pistil and stamen, cunt and clitoris. The poems are of the body, and the body is politically charged. There are stanzas that swing and spit: 'spare me dear reader / your knowing wink / that women's disfigurement / can be men's entertainment'; but there is laughter in defiance, and a playful linguistics at work:

see them adept
at ejecting lovers
who expect
sex
but have no rhymes for clitoris
('rhymes for clitoris')

Charman is a dissident whose poems are not compunctious in their offense. Her casual environmentalism sees her shooed from a fast-food premises:

well this is awkward
they've threatened to trespass me
from Carl's Jr
('waste management')

Other times, activism is brought back to a life beyond the political. In an attempt to save the 100-year-old Canal Road trees in Avondale:

some of us are arrested
which is for you
the goal of chemo
('ignore repeated word: delete repeated word')

Sometimes the 'i' is recognisable to us in its absence of heroics. It shoulders the weight of everything we wish we'd done but didn't do; it stands aside and watches the scenes pass us by; it is heedful of life's traumas but ultimately voiceless. Charman's 'thirteen bystanders' is a testimony of passivity. A witness.

revisit my teacherly turn of the head
as i graded your story
and did not look back
at the stains on the sleeping bag
to see how they got there
and what you'd said

Here Charman is a two-headed Janus, leaning in to the hardest truths, fetching us a hand mirror and confronting us with the cruellest versions of ourselves — and cooing to us, patting us on the shoulder when we catch a glimpse. She is a teacher, and she is a carer. She is jester and radical, mother and philosopher. This is a book of insurrection, but where pistils obviate any need for pistols. In her poem for Aung San Suu Kyi, Nobel Peace Prize laureate and once political prisoner, words are things of potency:

in these moist
interior rooms
leaves
in their warning flutters
remind me of books

to be set alight

Chris Holdaway

Chris Holdaway
Gorse Poems
Titus Books, 2022
RRP $25, 72pp

In *Gorse Poems* Chris Holdaway depicts a world in decay, physically and emotionally, a product of war, colonisation and commerce. The planet itself has been shaken — like tectonic plates, at the dinner table; it's washing up, getting sea-swamped like a desert island in the Pacific, and what are we gonna do about the disintegrative effects of colonisation, indestructible weed, land alienation? We are still here: the missionaries have turned into us. The ground is cleared for 'a smile of power lines under a rainbow . . . Markers of civilisation'; the war is over, but only 'In the way wind turbines are stationary'.

> and every lighthouse/A monument to who you were/
> not there for
>
> ('Floating point')

The poet meditates on the passing of generations, worlds; and new worlds, new civilisations built on the dust and waste products of us, where you reach into post-postmodern silence beneath dust, human waste-cum-housepaint. This could form the foundation for a new art, and we ourselves might be contemplated, as we contemplate those who came before us.

But what's the point of continuous building on the ruins of the past — the damp, the by-product of goldsweat? Where is the will to live? Do you not jump off merely because you 'Don't understand any of these buildings well / Enough' ('Heritage Pamphlet')? — Or because your friends don't jump; because they had the same idea, all at once, of not jumping off? Look instead for 'The eternity of features marked on maps that have / Gone . . .' — because all this junk is worthless: it slips 'between fingers like sand' ('Mataura').

The taonga, the real treasure, is something at once spiritual and tangible — something of a paradox, but real — more real than paper mills and freezing works that discharge their toxic effluent even. We ought to live for *community*, with the land — not for land exploitation, gold, real estate. All this has produced the 'age of machines', a world of 'pure / Numbers' ('Mataura'). How do we 'truly bridge water' ('Heritage Pamphlet')? — how to connect: with each other, our history, our future?

The bridge, the dominant motif in this collection, becomes a symbol of disconnection — from one place to nowhere, to nothing. It fails to connect, and hearts are linked only by 'the Platonic / Form of space between pylons' — which is nothing, really: shadows on a cave wall ('Sea Burial'). We are disconnected, like Hart Crane when he jumped ship and discovered Atlantis, or the Gulf of Mexico. We are dying, in our own quiet way, clocking out, staring up at the frozen sky of alien constellations, (dis)-figuring the patterns, joining the dots of Matariki, describing the arc from the Somme to Proxima Centauri. Cicadas are heard in winter and even the dioxide is dying.

These poems rage against the products and waste products of (Western) civilisation, the world of money-chasers, industrial and intensive agricultural development, birds swallowing plastic, and 'viable oil'. All of these things are denounced while the corresponding loss is lamented: nature, humanity, life. It is a 'protest over the paved-over trail of tears' ('Heritage Pamphlet'), measured by a pulse, the poetic rhythms that drive the moral. Holdaway wonders whether he relies 'too much / On . . . Hart Crane's frozen music — moments of collapse / Both change and stillness at once' ('Southwesterly Gorse'). Still, there's a light, 'Like the tiffany lamp glass towers that hide / so much dead stone in the night between / Lit up windows.'

'Treat yourself every so often to / Something that gives you the chance to ignite / The atmosphere — light *light* on fire'; discover the 'Connection that can begin from somewhere other / Than disruption':

This southless
Wind in privileged position to witness the decline
Of the fall of the West. To hope for so much that even
                                        undoing appears at risk of extinction.
('Southwesterly Gorse')

Mark Prisco

Richard von Sturmer

Richard von Sturmer
Resonating Distances
Titus Books, 2022
RRP $30, 150pp

Richard von Sturmer has written a beautiful and poignant collection of 50 short poems, each one thematically accompanied by a short story, a flash of myth and memory. The whole collection is strung together by a series of interconnecting themes, motifs, images and impressionistic recall: spiderwebs, cicada shells, floor sanders fading from a building site as you walk away; raindrops, the 'rustling of a . . . thrush' — the passing sensations of life ('1.5'). At night it's like forgetting, like a fever vibrating in your bones, and there's

> one black thought
> for each inch of infinity.
> ('1.9')

All the old stuff of our childhood is dying, is dead. Shut down, overexposed. This feels like post-war apocalypse. Possibly we're just characters in a story, heading for the supermarket with its supply of meat still in the freezers. There's post-facto irony in the billboard poster: our future is in space! ('5.8') The humans are in space, all right, one way or another. Probably in the form of dust:

> From childhood to old age, our lifespan is as brief as a shooting star in the mid-winter sky, or the flickering light of a firefly as it makes its way
> across a
> summer lawn.
> ('1.5')

To be or not to be is not the question, and the rottenness isn't just at the heart of Denmark, but at the heart of everywhere and everything ('1.5'). There is no question, and if there was, the answer is: *Not to be* — in the end. There is no closure. No healing. Except Not being.

Death. The fox is coming, and even your name will disappear. What is left 'In this empty/cicada-shell world . . .

> thousands of dark rooms
> each emitting its own level
> of low-frequency pain.
> ('2.5')

From the midst of desolation and loneliness comes a revelation — but it's the light of the moon on the white hand basin: whiteness increased by whiteness, a nullity: we have no memory; it's as if we came from nowhere, an oblivion of sea. We feel disconnected, and it's hard to distinguish between dreams and not dreams. Our memories are like mist; reside on the farther side of our thinking. And we all feel the pain of loss, the growing zero inside the chest ('5.10').

Mr Hasegawa has had a heart attack and meditates on the meaning of existence as he waits for the ambulance. He can smell the white night-blooming moonflowers outside his window. Then the ambulance arrives:

> Its revolving blue light revolved around the living room ceiling. A
> beautiful
>   shade
> of blue, thought Mr Hasegawa . . .
> ('4.10')

That 'beautiful shade of blue' is but a small crack in the vastness of death. Does it let the light in? Might we be rewarded by a 'patchwork of sunlight shining on the fields of rice'? ('5.9') It takes patience to construct something, whether house or landscape, from solid materials or out of air; to understand the poetry in a heap of corrugated iron, rusted nails, to capture the light of mudflats as the tide goes out, to see beauty in the old man hammering out his last book ('3.5'); the poetry of an empty house where

> downstairs swallows flit
> from room to room
> ('3.7')

Meanwhile, the hard rain darkens the brickwork and the flower pots. There's washing on the line, waves as high as castle walls, and love fades to a faint smile. Also, a friend has died, and we ourselves are turning 60 ('4.3' and '4.4'). The view of the human condition gets darker — in Pasolini's film, in the reality of his brutal murder ('3.10'). Von Sturmer wants the beauty of the world to overwhelm the evil, the horror — a world in which all is well, as it should be, where no one is killed, and a happy dog wags its tail, or lies beside us sleeping, a reassurance that fills the physical — or metaphysical gap, which is a sort of homelessness of the soul.

And why not. To hear the church bell! To lie, to die in an open field. We might contemplate the mirror on the ocean floor where fish see themselves as flames ('2.7').

Scott Hamilton

Scott Hamilton
Sonnets for Sio
Titus Books, 2022
RRP $25, 72pp

Scott Hamilton's collection of poetry is structured around a series of correspondences (real or imagined) with his friend Visesio Siasau (Sio), a carver, sculptor, painter and poet. Its settings range from the lounge of a tourist-infested hotel in Nuku'alofa to the first day of Creation; and, along the way, New York, an art gallery in Australia, the fifteenth-century geography of Kau'ulufonuafekai's violent incursions, and the Tongan Underworld, where the dead skulls roast pigs on the eternal flames and chew kava. We are at one moment descending into a primordial world of intense colour, before the world (or Word) had meaning, and the next in Manhattan, where 'Snotdrops of rain hang from the eves of cab stands' ('37') — or in the poet's room staring at the 'white desert' of blank paper, waiting for the poem ('9').

Hamilton navigates his way through the variegated real and meta landscapes like an antipodean Odysseus (or Ulysses) traversing the kava-dark waves — of the seas, or the detritus of inner-city modern living and death, where history, art and myth mingle with the stench of fisherman piss, with the blood of enemies, beggars on a bench or crackpots claiming hollow worlds, brains worked over by the Masonic Lodge. We could be in a plush hotel on a Pacific island where it's 31 degrees outside, or wandering the dark streets of Joyce's Dublin. Either way, we descend the 'dark dark dark' — 'Like Milton, like Eliot' — searching with a flashlight 'for another box of beers' ('13').

All time seems to exist simultaneously, and all places are one place only. The poet interweaves, skilfully, the connecting threads that hold us together, the spirits that abide beneath our surfaces, that rise at the very moment when our eyes are blind to it, who will not '*surrender / to analysis*' ('36'). Hamilton's collection is held together by the very anomalies, the violent contrasts, that would splinter into a universe of disparate atoms, that reconnect, perhaps, in a single brick within which lies, if not the entire universe, the cracked ceramics and all the kitsch paraphernalia of 1983 ('29').

Anything could happen. Marx might wash up on the shore, as Denis Glover emerges in the gaunt daylight of Vuna Road ('32'). You might see Satan (or his bro Sisu/Jesus) dozing on the beach, getting tanned. What else is there to do after you've risen from the bowels of hell and crucified the world? ('53') You might, I suppose, hang out with other gods in a coffee house, or shoot pool 'in the rec room / of the Ballarat Motor Camp' ('22').

There seems to be an unwholesome coincidence of things — of tanpura strings that, like cicadas, make silence audible, the empty escalators carrying the spirits into our world where the Manukau throws up on Cornwallis pier ('31'). There's the ugly conjunction of religion with the expedient requirements of modernity, 'the engine . . . working / in concert with your prayers' ('26'). There is war, moreover. Alternatively, there is the threat of war. Once, the Japanese were the enemy, now the archaeologists defend their trenches against deckchair invaders armed with 'slabs of beer' ('46'). The fire waits in the inert branches of alders ('38'). Beneath the mundane is a latent hell, and 'The Waikato river doesn't care / whether it carries a cadaver or a curious man' ('8').

There is invasion, the violence of warlords and British colonialists, the vulgar incursions of up-town culture and mod-cons, the castration of nature, von Tempsky, drunk, pissing in the ditch ('39'). The poet wants time erased, one feels, or rewound, the backward march of flagpoles turning back into trees ('41'); the world of book understanding, of metaphor and simile, dissolving like a lump of sugar into the reality of a cloud, and coconut trees — ancient pillars. Sleeping bats meanwhile squeal like the Athenian quorum when it 'honoured / Socrates / with its sentence of death' ('43' and '44').

These are bitter experiences. 'Mister Nakamura' smiles, counting the bubbles as he descends the depths of the Pacific, already dead, his sub struck, with the roar of water in his ears that might be applause ('48'). You slip off the boat into the sea, past algae, hardening into a snake, crawling up onto the sand towards the cold bonfire of Hikule'o, and the dancing skeletons ('57'). But there's an easy acceptance of fate, a faith in what's available, like the twinkling light of a cigarette in the dark ('45'). 'I praise the goddess because / she does not exist.' The whites — they offer the impossible: 'grace, redemption, evacuation' ('54').

> . . . Hikule'o's heaven
> is a hole filled with mud &
> maggots. I praise her
> with this mouth full of dirt.
> ('54')

Mark Prisco

This Twilight Menagerie

This Twilight Menagerie: A Whakanui of 40 Years of Poetry Live!
Edited by Jamie Trower and Sam Clements
Poetry Live!, 2021
RRP $28.99, 218pp

This Twilight Menagerie is a celebration of Poetry Live! — a weekly event in an Auckland pub where anyone can wander in from the street and recite a poem, if they're brave enough, and have something to say. In her introduction, Genevieve McClean recalls her first time behind the mic, after which a poet grabbed her by the shoulder and said 'Your poetry is as good as anyone else's!'

That sums up the democratic spirit of Poetry Live!, where the stench of booze and the occasional heckler mesh with the poet's dream of princes, 'beauty / strung like a broken guitar' (Heidi North); where the sound of the swill of beer competes with a roundelay of kitchen pots, blocked toilets and chemicals. You get flicked with a tampon, a bum wipe, assaulted by 'odours vaginal, fish-linger . . . condoms . . . HIS fingers' (Sophia Wilson). Or you get rolled by an acid blend of table talk and angle-fucked facts (Richard Taylor). It's a shit life but someone's got to live it, again.

I've never been to one of these events, but there must be quiet moments, too, where you feel the dead stir, into 'something *else* again' (Brian Flaherty), or a birdsong refrain (Jenny Clay). Beneath (and intertwined with) the flight path of David Eggleton's gazelles and jumbos — 'a stadium screaming now! now!' — and Jamie Trower's luminous joy of a dancer, there's an octopus intelligence, a vast impermeable consciousness that squeezes its way through the tight crevices of our imaginings, where we can be alone, immune to the 'noise' of our physical circumstances (Stephane Christie). 'Dear Sir', it's a dark world of 'words unsaid, / unsent, thriving on the blink / of her cursor' (Katie Millington) — a place, a time, that straddles the gap between what is said and what is felt (Richard Taylor), and the heaven of pain transcended (Stella Peg Carruthers). 'Please Go All The Way':

> *Behold her . . .*
> —
>
> pierced red inside her folds . . .
>   she sings herself whole
> (Anita Arlov)

'We rise and seek justice': 'meet me in the Underworld' (Emere Phoenix). You might find us in the piss grunge of a pub, reading a poem to an audience of rapt drunks, or squat amid the junk of a 'corrugated corner' beneath the dim glow of a '60-watt bulb' (Aidan Howard). We get ripped by the 'iron slick' experience, crushed by the hulk of metal, 'like a pomegranate is crushed into a sieve' (Luka Venter). I wish we were miles away, where you feel the late sun green through the vine, and there's the

> glow of crushed
> grape
> lifted up
> to our lips
> and
> drunk
> down to
> the dusks
> of evening
> (Peter Le Baige)

We could spend 'exactly a lifetime / half of which had looked like sky' (Genevieve McClean) — and notice there the heavenly ache, like freedom, the sense of our own emptiness.

Here's to you, brothers and sisters, to the warmth of community, 'a beaker full of the warm South . . . the blushful Hippocrene', and the isolate joy of our solitude.

Ora Nui 4

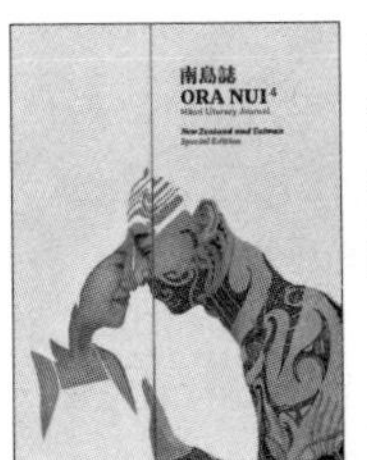

Ora Nui 4: Māori Literary Journal
Edited by Kiri Piahana-Wong and Shin Su
Oranui Press, 2021
RRP $45, 280pp

Ora Nui 4, edited jointly by Shin Su and Kiri Piahana-Wong, is an incredible work that draws out the whakapapa connections between Maaori and Taiwanese. Briefly, Maaori have their origins in Taiwan, from where, long ago, the Indigenous peoples of that place began to migrate outwards. The work in this book is of such a range, from short story and visual art to poetry to novel excerpt to photography to essay, that the threads that wind together are of so many different colours and focuses. This isn't just an attempt at tracing a connection, it's a space that has allowed these many artists to speak to their own worlds. The tying together of these connections is for the reader to attempt.

There are 50 contributors and I do not have the space here to touch on all of their work but I want to mihi to them all! As all these artists/writers have, I want to speak to my own specific journey within the book. This will be less a review and more a tracing of connections; a haerenga whakawhanaungatanga. A response to the person and the work neither in isolation, because these are people I know and love and to ignore that is just some white shit.

I'm going to start with Aziembry Aolani's 'Name'. The power of a name, the power of an identity. It speaks to a common reality for Indigenous peoples of what we've lost and where we have lost it and the past that swallows it up. 'Give me my name back, / decapitated, / on the rear of father's utility. / It has hosted rust since 1993'. Aolani is not just letting the world take their name, they are demanding it back, through everything. I met Aziembry at Te Haa and my impression of them was shy and thoughtful and I think of them often and sometimes let that thought become a quiet message on Facebook. I think of this poem and maybe that quietness is a determination to hold on to what we could still yet lose.

Like Aziembry, I met Cassandra Barnett at Te Haa, in her colourful playsuits with her wonderful son. Cassandra has this softness to her that makes you feel safe in koorero, but will never let a suss idea go unchallenged. We didn't talk much over Te Haa; our ties drew closer at the Brisbane Writers Festival, where we both ended up in quarantine in a hotel together. We Facetimed all of those seven days. Cass made me an apple crumble with ingredients scraped together from delivered groceries and the sugar sachets in her room. It is probably the best dessert I've ever had. It's moments like these that you know you are loved. This care and love that I have been shown is clear as day in her work.

The pain of a misunderstanding, of continuous misunderstandings; what does being Maaori look like, 'New World Jam' asks us. How it interacts with whiteness, how it interacts with blackness? How do we bring our children up so they know they are loved, how do we bring them up in a world where they are othered? And the 'Three Tanka' that follow this are glorious celebrations of life; of being in the water of 'manu the belly flop', 'cack-handed fringe swipe' of 'grinning stalk-eyed biker pup' of that 'electric deep'! Coming back to these words now, I live for the human heartbeat in them.

I met Kirsty Dunn at Word Festival in Ootautahi. I remember the exchange being brief, being thankful to meet in person. I remember her wearing black skinny jeans and a dark top. Was it a hoodie? My memory isn't that good. I think if anyone was to write a poem about the eel then it's got to be someone with such goth vibes. Her poem 'tuna', which I've carried with me since reading it for the first time years ago, is shaped like a tuna on the page and it moves like one. The way Dunn uses the reo to disrupt and evolve the English of the text, 'wears her / years her / whakapapa / her body / down'. Every time I read it I feel like I'm evolving, like some idea is coming closer to fruition. It also reminds me of my koro, whose middle name is Tuna; I think of him swimming through the night sky shifting and changing like this poem.

I remember Amber Esau from Auckland Writers Festival: all fabulous curls and fierce intelligence, us hanging out talking about Greek mythology and poetry while the rest got drunk on the stage, under a blue light, white people schmoozing over white tablecloths. I find her work so electric always. Just the start of 'Manaakitanga', 'With a shark's tooth / she skins an apple / and chucks the meat', is enough to get me excited: I can feel these words move through my body!

And the aforementioned Greek mythos evoked in a different context in 'Dancing the Siva Samoa': 'Watch Cerberus-threedog dance the Sāsā / slapping his chest, shoulders, / elbows, bend easy fish bones / they're sharp as tears / sometimes / our own a weapon fragile.' Esau's lines always bend and fold, and even when she's referencing across time and contexts the work feels stunningly embodied. And so often they come back to bones. Let us keep coming back to our bones and what grounds us in this crazy world.

Anahera Gildea is whanaunga, she comes from Tukorehe marae, the cousin of my own marae, Wehi Wehi. I found this out in a Facebook audio message, after telling her we both came from the same iwi. The audio fuzz and the excited response. And her reaching out to the Pacific in her piece feels as if it channels a similar desire to lay out these connections: 'a tsunami of movement — mihi to the peoples of the Pacific' speaks to the connection of our people to the natural world; 'our highways are wai ways / an oceanic swell / of dormant tongues / can strip lies from words / speak like your ancestors / measure yourself against the sky'. The play and movement reflecting the play and movement of the world. We have a history of being navigators, something the whole book speaks to. There is a power in this that can't be denied!

I met Kelly Joseph on campus, where we had coffee and sat at a table and talked about writing and being Maaori. We've grown closer over the years and I cherish the pounamu leaf earrings she bought me for my twenty-sixth (?) birthday. I heard her read at Poppies once and the cave and moa in her story stuck around. When I think of Kelly I think of warmth for people and a deep searching for answers to questions that maybe none of us have the answers to. Her story 'Obsidian Dream' is a story about displacement and what grounds us. Set on Turtle Island it somehow feels familiar even if I've never been to the States, am not a guy, and have never been tugged off in a pool. 'Obsidian Dream' pulls you into this world where things have all gone a little wrong; it explores how even when you're far away from home you're anchored by things and these things can feel complicated can feel like drags.

And they do for the main character and Maaori fellow far from home. In this case the drags are his mother's cancer and his father's panic attacks. In the last scene of the story he searches for the Southern Cross and can't find it and as someone who when they look to stars sees just incoherent light I couldn't relate more to this moment. How difficult it is to navigate having been turned around so often.

I think the first time I saw Kahu Kutia was on Instagram as @hinenuitehoha. I thought that name was sick and that their art was incredible, too. They did a reinterpretation of Princess Mononoke as Maaori and so I followed them. We met in person long after we knew of each other; at the Waikato Museum, we walked through the Star Gossage exhibit together, marvelling at her art, so many-layered and spectral. Kahu has an indomitable spirit, they find hope and power in many things others would find crushing.

'I decide to go all out at this point. About be roadkill anyway' is the thought of the main character in their story 'Kids' but could so easily represent Kahu's worldview. I love the world she crafts in this piece, it feels like that space of adolescence where everyone is pretending to be older than they are. But I think this is a pretending we should return to more often because in it the world opens up and things that felt impossible can just be done. Kahu teaches me that.

'Blood brothers' by Anne-Marie Te Whiu is a piece that haunts me. Who has the time to want the things we're 'supposed' to want as Maaori? 'I recite a karakia for my brothers / they would prefer I bring kebabs': it gets me thinking about all the material needs our people have before they can reclaim even an ounce of what others say is Maaoritanga.

I met Anne-Marie Te Whiu at Te Haa, but I would say the first time we properly connected in person was years later at the Brisbane Writers Festival. I remember being so incredibly tired from the travelling and her excitement carried me from room to room and from person to person. She is so unbelievably giving and her enthusiasm for life and care for others is an energy I wish I could emulate even a tiny percentage of!

'Kewpie' by Stacey Teague is a delicate exploration of death and connection, about their kui who has passed on. It describes seeing her 'body displayed in the house for three days' and reminds me of seeing my koro lying in the wharenui underneath the kurii with the giant dick. Where was he in there? 'Her body like an ocean with nothing beneath.' Death is fucking weird. We sit with these once animated bodies and expect them to turn their heads and say something like: nice to see you again moko, hope you're keeping out of trouble moko, what poems have you written moko? Before this poem is over I feel like I know this woman, maybe more than I knew my koro; 'She liked the TV show, *Pingu*,' same here, kui, same here.

I met Stacey at Browsers bookshop in Hamilton. I remember they were thinking about going to do a master's at the IIML and wondered if I had any advice. I have no memory of what I said in response. Stacey has a way of cocking her head to one side when listening that could look judgmental, but when she does it it feels opening, as if she's really listening. Our first exchange was earlier through *Scum Mag*, a journal she edits where she published my poem 'ECHIDNA GOES OUT ON THE TOWN: MEETS TYPHON'.

Michelle Rahurahu says the first poem they read of mine was that one, the one Stacey published. Do I have Stacey to thank for this friendship? I don't know. I met Michelle on Twitter: them and a friend, Sinead, were putting together a thread of poetic responses to Ihumaatao. I suggested we put together a book. And that is how we became friends, we put together a fucking book, the waa always got to do things on hard mode. Along with Ruby Solly, Hana Pera Aoake and Sinead Overbye: all takataapui Maaori trying to bring together responses in the moment.

The first time we hung out in person Michelle gifted me Tamawahine, a patu, to hold. It had been broken that morning but its wairua was transferred to this vessel. I think of our friendship like that, firm greenstone with fractured insides. Coz we're both people with fractured insides. The first time we hung out just to hang out was for the launch of *Poetry New Zealand Yearbook 2020*. It feels fitting that our friendship comes back here.

In my copy of *Ora Nui* Michelle's piece 'The Children of the Fern', as something of a tradition, is covered in markup and drawings I got them to do in lieu of just a regular signature. On one page is a tear dropping into a dark pool, another paragraph is highlighted with the phrase 'italicise' next to it, elsewhere they make a remark about not using double vowels like a staunch Raukawa. 'The Children of the Fern' is the conceptualising of a childhood through the form of puuraakau. The whole poem feels like an ancient story, but as with all puuraakau they reflect on the time they were told and the contexts of the storyteller.

There is trauma here and pain, of familial violence and rape. I think about my own sexual beginnings, so different from the ones depicted here, but still shrouded in that category of *incest*. A thing we can never talk about. A thing that stops us from talking about the cycles of violence that continue in our families and homes. This piece doesn't shrink from any of it. Rahurahu uses the style of the puuraakau, of its lofty tone and pushes into it, exposes the trauma to the light: 'the whole world is made of open wounds / she wants to go to the night / wants to see the dark swell again'.

And maybe there are answers here in the willingness to go back into that dark and pluck something out of it. I think back to the story of Hinetetama and Taane Mahuta. I think back to my brother just giving me a 'massage'. I think to all the ways in which we carry pain. The millions of decisions that mean we pass it on, or it dies with us. What pain travels along our whakapapa, and does it all stem from that one man landing his boat here in 1769? The spinning of time. We are our ancestors, but were our ancestors always good? What ways can things be spun out of a spiral? What pain can we heal, what pain can we let go of? 'oh poor oh poor / poor fern / unfurling in the centre of the storm'.

At the end of the poem you leave me a written message, Michelle, and I'm not sure if you'll remember this, that says 'hope this tale inspires lots of tears e hoa' and it has and it will, as your story spins in and out of mine. In contrast to the tears, I remember us laughing about the spelling of your name on the back of the book which turned Rahurahu into Rahu Rahu, two baskets, one for each of us, to pile increasingly deranged jokes into.

With all that said, this book is itself a basket of knowledge, of so many different stories and perspectives that trace an unknowable and gigantic whakapapa. And inside this whakapapa so many connections have been made. I am so thankful for it.

Rebecca Hawkes

Rebecca Hawkes
Meat Lovers
Auckland University Press, 2022
RRP $25, 92pp

If you're accustomed to picking up a poetry collection, getting two pieces in and declaring, 'Ahh yes, very reminiscent of X and Y author's early period', I dare you to try that here. The cover of *Meat Lovers* should tip you off that Rebecca Hawkes' first standalone collection is a plethora of unique and textural viscera. She has always been a poet whose work feels fresh and gorgeously unconventional. As someone who has enjoyed and followed Hawkes' work for years, it's a thrill to be holding a book of purely her. And there is no let-down. From start til close, you are served up blood and fairies, friendship and gore, 'gumboots and lace', all strung together with a remarkably astute eye.

But before we get sucked into the poetry proper, we need to talk about the cover. Life, death and sexuality are front and centre with luscious and nigh-on bacchanalian imagery. The reds and pinks make the cover almost shocking compared to its counterparts. It's the kind of book to leave on the coffee table to alarm your father, or to initiate an interesting conversation when bringing a first date back to yours. And the title certainly prompts consideration — are they lovers made of meat, lovers of meat, or are they lovers who love meat? Is meat inextricably tied with love, or are they completely separate because being brought together would highlight a cultural perversion we can't look in the eye?

Then there are the gumboots. Those iconic Red Band farm staples are on the feet of two women, whose thighs are subtly marbled like expensive steak. The bloody moon, the mist, the blue-tinted figures turn this scene into an alien, supernatural landscape, with sucker tendrils and carnivorous plants pushing it further. We are classic New Zealand but on Venus, where a pavlova spills pitcher plants and blooded lip prints adorn a goblet of milk.

Meat Lovers is a collection of two halves, 'Meat' and then 'Lovers'. The opening piece, 'The Flexitarian', is heavily referenced by readers of the collection and it is clear why. Beginning as a trip to the supermarket, it encapsulates themes and images to which the following pieces will speak. It's meat as sexualised recrimination; blood as lipstick, and a pig nipple winks, weeps and bubbles in the hot pan, wringing forth a severe discomfort in the reader. It's a strong choice for the opening poem, and the final line, 'Blisters where I burn my tongue on it', makes it clear that *Meat Lovers* is going deep and dirty into whatever subjects it likes, even if they're the sort we don't normally enjoy witnessing in cohabitation.

Early poems dance through girlhood; there's supermarket pick 'n' mix with mum, school buses and pony clubs, but with hints of dead animal and unquenched thirst. It's not until 'Flesh tones' that we are on the farm, and the girl's world is one 'made on the music of meat'.

A recurrence throughout the collection is the narrator as animals and in different skins — especially in a piece there isn't space to discuss ('The Protagonists'). Noticeably, as we go into the warm lambs' tails in sacks, paddock stillbirths, and the sad ethical ambiguity of 'Is it cruelty?', the anthropomorphic shifts of the narrator relate to forms of predator not prey. This aspect seems to reflect a mismatch in the pragmatic, pastoral world and the wilder, emotive hidden skin of the girl.

It's a challenge to not address nearly every poem in the 'Meat' half — there's so much feeling displayed in dazzling excess as well as in quiet scenes with deep implications. The yellow of gorse blooms pop, there's 'hot milk' flowing, and so much snow in her boots that 'the frost felt hot'. The moral quandaries stick to your fingers as you turn the pages. 'The Conservationist' sees four helpless kittens nestled in a tree stump and a narrator with a gentle heart who knows they will be murderers if allowed to reach adulthood. And the voice from 'Is it cruelty?' is hard to shake even when the book is closed. A question is asked near the end of the section, and the collection asks it in other ways, too: 'if there was a world without suffering / could you be happy in it'.

The 'Lovers' section is shorter but no less captivating. We are inside a maturing and experimental perspective. The poems begin with girlhood finding womanhood in a world of sexualities, mythical animals and the phase of the 'low-production-value manic pixie budget goth regime'. The hard-fall infatuation of female love in 'Undeliverance' is relatable enough to hurt. Hawkes melds meat, fantasy and relationships into a concoction which should be jarring or chaotic, but instead creates a breathing and multi-faceted humanity that will make you laugh and cry.

'Grazing platter' brings the two halves of the collection together. Being nearly at the close of 'Lovers', the piece shows that while the girl is a woman in the city, she has not become the soft archetype who can't touch raw chicken. Two halves, which society likes to separate, are brought together inside her; the two girls housed in one skin. And it's simply fantastic. The final stanza reads:

> I am preparing for the impact
> where my prosecco glass meets
> the flashy granite countertop
> I will slit necks with the shards
> and drink and drink and drink my fill

Hawkes' writing, even when talking about love and loss, does not lose the edge of her uncanny gore.

Meat Lovers does what all good poetry should, it sits us down with truth and does not allow us to re-circulate the air, instead forcing us to 'breathe the evidence'. It gives us visceral thrills, puts fur between our teeth, tells us of plans to feed the landlords to erotic carnivorous plants and, with the poem 'Sighting', reminds us that there's always a lover deep inside us, thirsty for an ampersand.

Dadon Rowell

AUP New Poets 8

AUP New Poets 8
Edited by Anna Jackson
Auckland University Press, 2021
RRP $29.99, 120pp

It is always intriguing to pick up an *AUP New Poets* collection — you don't know where you're going to be transported, but you know it'll be sensational. *AUP New Poets 8* vibrates with talent, and thus poses an issue to review. I've had the pleasure of reading Lily Holloway and Modi Deng in the fabulous *Starling*, so I knew I would adore their sections. Tru Paraha was a name I'd seen around but not really read, then several pieces deep into her section, I got to:

> thigh bone pavilion
> en
> tangle tan angel
> staccato g-s pots
> dreamtime broth
> ('A. sky')

I had to take the book over to show my partner, whose response was, 'she is so fucking good' — to which I had to wail, 'I know, they all are.' This is not to make the review into some kind of myopic piece which is actually all about the reviewer, but to stress how special this collection is. When you hold the work of three poets in your hands at once, the sheer skill and mahi strikes you. The poets — introduced by Anna Jackson's incredibly attuned foreword — wow, sizzle and hit you with quiet melodies that play out long after you have finished reading.

Holloway opens, with her section named 'a child in that alcove'. Her first piece is slim and pared back, effortlessly reflecting the spinal 'divots' which she references. It is evident Holloway is a skilled poet, and the closing line is an image, movingly expressed, which perfectly places the reader to receive the following collection:

> It happens
> and a child
> runs backwards
> rewinding
> into
> my chest.
> ('Reverb or Aftermath')

'a child in that alcove' is full of imagery, texture and sensation. Rivers and tides match with reverberations and call-back voices. Some pieces are soft, others thoughtful, still more cut deeply with loud or acute lines. The form of the words on the page shifts, becoming more mobile as the collection progresses. Much of this serves to ramp up, in the first half, to the pull-no-punches, gorgeously stunning intensity of 'you are my night terror i hope i am yours'.

Holloway has a knack for getting a bodily response from the reader; mouths are open for all number of things to spill or crawl out; slugs and insects slime and flitter along the margins. The final piece fragments totally, and is the perfect way for Holloway to end her section, leaving white space for Paraha's entrance.

Tru Paraha's 'in my darkling universe' opens strongly, with a confidently vivid voice. The stochastic formatting mixed with te reo and computer language within a collection about universe beginnings is a heady combination. Parts of it are reminiscent of essa may ranapiri's *ransack*, speaking to the fraught nature of language in the digital age. I don't say this to detract from Paraha's being wholly unique. She carries the flavour of a poet who knows what she is doing, and has epic control over the page. There are some incredible lines early on, with 'infinitely compressed bright meat' and 'thigh bone pavilion', but they don't quite prepare you for the stomach-deep cough you give when you reach page 54: 'the golds could've been scraped off Cleopatra's vulva'. Now that is a line. A pause, sit back, reach for a glass of water line. The piece brims with images and multiple levels of emotion, and shows how Paraha melds depth, temporal cultures and, at times, a perfect level of irreverence.

About midway through, a wall-of-text page appears, featuring facts about 'participant y' with the occasional redacted black line. The poem is justified and clearly pushing at the seams, giving both a sense of enforced confinement and stubborn defiance. Voice and character come through so clearly, humanly and often amusingly: 'participant y assumes a champagne lifestyle on a beer budget' and 'participant y has friends in low places'.

Modi Deng brings us back to earth from Paraha's final astronaut, in a way which feels gentle and intimate. 'an wei' (to use the transliteration Deng provides) moves us through time and sits with us in sublime, sincere moments. The first piece, 'lessons', shows us the worlds Deng's poems move through. It includes how to breathe during a performance, nineties-era Keri Russell, and the especially poignant line 'the air softly eats up words when we / break our hearts in-between'. Melodic flow and aural techniques carry us through the images of Deng's work, until we are the ones hiding the desecration of Beethoven's piano and 'texting boys test answers'.

One of the most touching and honest pieces of the whole collection is 'a conversation'. It is a little tricky to recreate the format, which is essentially split like a back-and-forth, so you will just have to find the original. It begins, 'my mother is not the type / to witness crying / and soften / to rush over / fluffy with concern / because she knows / each state is only a / liquid'. This piece spoke to one of Holloway's lines, in a way that moved me intensely but I find hard to articulate, Holloway's being: 'i am healing a deep slow burn'. The sense of a narrator growing, exploring where they are from, where they are going, and how to ford the distance feels very present.

AUP New Poets 8 is a stunning collection, alive with three different voices and their stories. The poets stand out as unique but also speak with each other on those central human truths. And in a collection this strong, covering childhood, family, creation and language, it feels fitting to end on these lines of Deng's: 'she was promised that when she reached eighteen / she'd unfurl herself / into a butterfly / instead she hardened like sugar'.

David Wrigley

Michael Steven / Chris Tse

Michael Steven
Night School
Otago University Press, 2022
RRP $25, 84pp

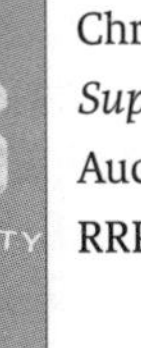

Chris Tse
Super Model Minority
Auckland University Press, 2022
RRP $24.99, 104pp

Where do we begin to look for the poet within a poem? Can we find her squatting among the cantilevered architecture of the black line, or dissolving into the terrible space of the blank page? Do we join him in the many-levelled houses of his psyche, complete with hobgoblin-infested basements, false floors and secret doors? Do we sit with them in sun-dappled glades, on wind-beaten beaches, in the stirring city at first light, or upon the ocean floor, engulfed in an eyeless gloom? Or perhaps the poet is not there at all. Perhaps the magician has made himself disappear in a puff of pale blue smoke, a suggestion, a perfect koan of misdirection.

Reading Te Whanganui-a-Tara poet Chris Tse's new collection *Super Model Minority* and Tāmaki Makaurau-based Michael Steven's *Night School* side by side, these questions of presence and corporeality seem vital. The two collections encapsulate Nietzsche's dichotomy between the Apollonian and the Dionysian impulses in the act of creation. The Apollonian is airy, cerebral and reasoned, with a clear delineation between the self and the other, the subject and the object.

The Dionysian is earthy, sensual, and chaotic, and characterised by a blurring of the boundaries between subject and object, what Nietzsche referred to as primordial unity. The question is: Do poets get to decide which god they will worship? Or do the accidents of their birth, their identities and their privileges force them, as matters of survival, to embrace the dissolution of Dionysus or accept the protection of Apollo?

Steven's collection *Night School* is a tapestry of dropped pins. East Auckland; Addington, Christchurch; Hāwera, South Taranaki; Razorback Road, Pōkeno. We pursue him in great zigzags across the country, the markers planted in real locations, mapping out not just space but also time, the poet's time, inner time. Wherever we go the poet is there with us between the lines, his senses working for us, showing us where we are. In Maramarua, East Waikato, 'mornings came thick with blanket fog, / the tang of diesel, the spice of pipe tobacco'. On a soon to be destroyed Pigeon Mountain, Pakuranga, East Auckland, 'you could pick buckets of wild mushrooms. / My father browned them off in butter and garlic'. Sensory details are gathered and dropped like breadcrumbs for us to follow.

As befits a collection called *Night School*, a quiet preoccupation with class runs through these poems. The night school in question is briefly alluded to — an electrical engineering class at Manukau Polytechnic, his classmates 'dropouts, baby dopers and drinkers'— but the real learning happens 'after work from psychonauts'. The wisdom of druggies and hard-cases abounds, there are cockies and slaughterers, sparkies and pilled-out ravers, 'Dave with his spade beard, / snarling', 'Whoever controls the weather / is the master of our emotions.' Steven is ever the autodidact, reading 'Kerouac, Camus and Blake' but also giving equal educational weight to 'GZA's solo album, *Liquid Swords*'.

He guides us through the precise geographies that have shaped him. Time is a much more flexible and mercurial medium. The many strains of weed for which half a dozen of these poems are named, the meth, the MDMA, the acid, the beer, all lend a Dionysian looseness to our illusionary sense of linear time. Steven's father 'threads the black steering wheel / of a dead man's ride'. He is there on that demolished mountain, picking mushrooms. His great-grandfather stares out of a photograph with 'the pathological terror, the ancestral dread' and Steven feels the past looping and repeating under the influence of amphetamines, 'the same terror / ringing out across time'. Drugs cause the boundaries of the self to dissolve, leaving only traces and spores of a sensual existence and the ripples of inherited trauma across the surface of time's strange ocean.

In *Super Model Minority*, Chris Tse's sense of place is fractured and illusionary. In 'In denial', he tells us 'Sometimes you can't tell the sky / apart from the hills — the more / you look, the more you begin to / doubt that either exists'. We rarely smell what he smells, touch what he touches, see what he sees. As Tse says in the coruscating 'Mike & Karl & Duncan & Martin', 'Nowhere is safe'.

Tse's presence within the poems is ethereal, cerebral, virtual; all the better to stay out of reach. His rage is there 'each time one of our brothers or sisters is / dragged into the news lifeless', his 'shadow cast onto the scene below', but for the sake of survival, his flesh is absent. His only recourse to the injustice that surrounds him is to 'march onto the internet with a fist raised high / and look them in the bylines, unblinking'.

Chris Tse is a voice: Apollonian, cut-glass, both furious and ironic. When he describes acts of the body, they are metaphorical acts, they are illustrations, interpretive dances. They are thoughts made flesh. 'I've eaten the words you told me I couldn't say. I've torn them / from your hands with my savage teeth and shredded them.' His art spins rage into the violence of metaphor, and the violences of the material world are transfigured, fleetingly, into

> art that moves us yet
> we know we can't enjoy — a bloody knife
> protruding from a portrait of a young gay man
> beaten to death
> ('In Denial')

as if to make looking at them bearable for just long enough to bear witness.

It is telling that when Tse does appear bodily within his poems it is in safe, protected spaces. His 'sunburnt neck / pulsed with residual heat or perhaps it was the spark / of memory' as he remembers watching George Michael perform at Sydney Mardi Gras and grieves for the singer in a car in Lower Hutt, his body remembering the ecstasy of belonging.

Similarly, in 'What's fun until it gets weird?' the poet is present (although perhaps mercifully in the second person) as he tries to explain the 'ethics and etiquette of bukkake' to his mother and aunties. It is, of course, excruciating, but it is also a poem filled with a quiet love, in which the only consequences are searing embarrassment and eye-contact avoided in the cereal aisle.

These collections, read side by side, remind us that time and memory are intimately entangled with the spaces we inhabit, that the spores of violence and trauma are scattered on every plane and surface, and that it is the work of poets to root them out, expose them and ultimately interpret them as either signpost or warning.

Contributors

Pip Alfeld is a copywriter, poet and artist based in Ōtautahi Christchurch. She skates, creates and cares for her debilitated father, with whom she reminisces about their days in the bush.

John Allison is a Ōtautahi Christchurch-based poet and the author of six poetry collections. His poem 'Father's Axe, Grandfather's Machete' was selected as one of 25 for *Ōrongohau | Best New Zealand Poems 2020*. His poem sequence 'The Poetics of Water' has been set to music for a chamber ensemble by Pieta Hextall, with whom he is collaborating on a choral work.

Aimee-Jane Anderson-O'Connor was the featured poet in *Poetry New Zealand Yearbook 2021*. She was awarded the 2018 Charles Brasch Young Writers' Essay Prize and was the co-winner of the 2017 Monash Undergraduate Prize for Creative Writing. Her work has appeared in a number of literary journals, including *Starling, Mayhem, Landfall, brief, Turbine | Kapohau, Verge* and *Minarets Journal.*

Hana Pera Aoake (Ngāti Hinerangi, Ngāti Mahuta, Tainui/Waikato, Ngāti Waewae) is an artist and writer. They work with Morgan Godfery on the publishing and education project kei te pai press. Hana published their first book, *A bathful of kawakawa and hot water*, with Compound Press in 2020.

Maia Armistead is a law student at Te Herenga Waka Victoria University of Wellington. She has been published in *Starling, Mayhem, Rejection Letters* and on *The Spinoff.*

Jane Arthur is a poet, editor and bookshop owner who lives in Pōneke Wellington. She won the Sarah Broom Poetry Prize in 2018, and her debut collection, *Craven* (Te Herenga Waka University Press, 2019) won the Jessie Mackay Prize for a best first book of poetry at the 2020 Ockham New Zealand Book Awards. Her second collection will be published in 2023.

Jayne Ault is a year 13 student at Wellington Girls' College. Their poem 'William II' won first prize in the 2022 *Poetry New Zealand Yearbook* Student Poetry Competition.

Rebecca Ball is a teacher based near Ōtautahi Christchurch. She has been published in journals including *Landfall, London Grip, Turbine | Kapohau* and *Poetry New Zealand Yearbook*, as well as in *More than a Roof* and *No Other Place to Stand.*

Holly H. Bercusson was born and raised in Tāmaki Makaurau Auckland with a love of letters. Add to that a complicated childhood, a personality disorder, a dash of Jewish neuroticism and you pretty much have a poet.

Tony Beyer lives in Taranaki. Among his print titles, *Anchor Stone* (Cold Hub Press, 2017) was a finalist in the poetry category of the 2018 Ockham New Zealand Book Awards. More recently, his work has appeared internationally including in *Allegro, Catalyst, London Grip, Mayhem, Mudlark, Otoliths, Social Alternatives* and *Tarot.*

Tyla Harry Bidois is a Jewish poet, author, illustrator and musician from Mount Maunganui. Her work centres largely on poetic form, womanhood and the exploration of mixed-race cultural identity. She has been published in *Mayhem* and *Poetry New Zealand Yearbook*, and her poetry collection *So Much Sky* was published in 2020.

Victor Billot is an Ōtepoti Dunedin-based writer. His poetry collection *The Sets* (Otago University Press) was published in 2021. He writes a weekly satirical ode on current affairs for *Newsroom*.

J. E. Blaikie is a graduate of the International Institute of Modern Letters at Te Herenga Waka Victoria University of Wellington. Her collection *Tongue Burglar* (Steele Roberts Aotearoa) was published in 2018.

Peter Bland is a poet and actor whose writing commits to an everyday sub-urban sense of reality, often exploiting the framework of the dramatic monologue. He was a co-founder of Downstage and its artistic director from 1964 to 1968. He has published a large selection of poetry volumes in New Zealand and the UK, and his memoir was released in 2004.

Cindy Botha began writing later in life, after six decades of doing other things. She is published in New Zealand, UK and US.

Iain Britton is an Aotearoa New Zealand poet and author of several poetry collections. His work has been nominated in the UK for a Forward Prize for Best Single Poem and Best First Collection. *The Intaglio Poems* was published by Hesterglock Press in 2017, and a new chapbook, *Project Constellation*, was published by Sampson Low in 2022.

Mark Broatch is a journalist, critic and the author of four books. He works as the books editor at the *New Zealand Listener*.

Owen Bullock's most recent books are *Uma rocha enorme que anda à roda* (A big rock that turns around), translations of tanka into Portuguese by Francisco Carvalho (Temas Originais, 2021), *Summer Haiku* (Recent Work Press, 2019) and *Work & Play* (Recent Work Press, 2017). He teaches creative writing at the University of Canberra.

Danny Bultitude has been published in several New Zealand journals and on websites, including *Ōrongohau | Best New Zealand Poems*, *Landfall*, *The Spinoff*, and *Poetry New Zealand Yearbook*. He recently completed his first novel and is still hunting for purpose in life.

Jessie Burnette is currently working to complete a master's degree in English at University of Waikato Te Whare Wānanga o Waikato. Her work has been published in *Mayhem* and *Poetry New Zealand Yearbook*.

Nathaniel Calhoun lives in the Far North of Aotearoa. He works with teams that monitor and restore biodiversity in ecosystems around the world. He has published or has upcoming work in *New York Quarterly*, *Guest House*, *takahē*, *Azure*, *DMQ Review*, *Misfit*, *Quadrant*, *Hawaii Pacific Review* and *Landfall*.

Brent Cantwell is a New Zealand writer originally from Tīmaru, who now lives with his family in the hinterland of Queensland, Australia. He teaches high school English and has been writing for 24 years. He has recently been published in *Poetry New Zealand Yearbook, Blue Nib, Australian Poetry Journal, foam:e* and *Landfall.*

Ella Cartwright (Ngāpuhi) grew up in Tokoroa and lives in Te Whanganui-a-Tara Wellington with her partner and two children. She writes poems about culture, whakapapa and whānau life.

Cadence Chung is a poet, student and musician from Te Whanganui-a-Tara Wellington, who is studying at the New Zealand School of Music Te Kōkī. She draws inspiration from Tumblr posts, antique stores and dead poets.

David Čiurlionis is currently completing a master's in creative writing at the University of Auckland Waipapa Taumata Rau. He has been published in *Mayhem* and *Newsroom.*

Imé Corkery is a poet by choice and chronic illness warrior by design. She loves to write about things she has been told not to write about.

harold coutts is a poet and writer based in Te Whanganui-a-Tara Wellington. They have been published in *Starling, Ōrongohau | Best New Zealand Poems, Poetry New Zealand Yearbook* and in the queer anthology *Out Here* (Auckland University Press, 2021).

Mary Cresswell is from Los Angeles and lives on the Kāpiti Coast. Her poems are in various journals in Aotearoa New Zealand, US, UK, Australia and Canada.

Vicky Curtin is an artist and teacher based in Waikato. She has previously published poetry in *Poetry New Zealand Yearbook* and *Mayhem.*

Jodie Dalgleish is a writer, curator, critic and sound artist based in Luxembourg. Her poetry has been published in *Landfall, Shearsman, Long Poem Magazine, Poetry Salzburg Review, Azure* and *Les Cahiers Luxembourgeois.* She holds a master's in creative writing from Auckland University of Technology Te Wānanga Aronui o Tāmaki Makaurau.

Piers Davies is a long-time poet and script writer who has published widely in Aotearoa New Zealand and overseas. He coordinates the group Titirangi Poets and co-edits their ezines and anthologies.

Brecon Dobbie finds poetry to be her place of solace. She writes to make sense of things, often without meaning to. Her work has appeared in *Starling, min-a-rets, Love in the time of COVID* and *Poetry New Zealand Yearbook.*

Leah Dodd is a poet and writer based in Pōneke Wellington. In 2021 she completed a master's with distinction at the International Institute of Modern Letters, where her collection won the Biggs Family Prize in Poetry. Her debut collection will be published by Te Herenga Waka University Press in 2023.

Doc Drumheller has worked in award-winning groups for theatre and music and has published 10 collections of poetry. His poems are translated into more than 20 languages, and he is the editor and publisher of the New Zealand literary journal *Catalyst*. His latest collection, *Drinking With Li Bai: 100 Haiku from China and India*, was published by Cold Hub Press in 2022.

David Eggleton is a recipient of the Janet Frame Literary Trust Award for Poetry, an Ockham New Zealand Book Award for Poetry, and the Prime Minister's Award for Poetry. He was the New Zealand Poet Laureate 2019–2022. His new book *Respirator: A Laureate Collection, Poems 2019 to 2022* will be published by Otago University Press in 2023.

Amber Esau is a Sā-māo-rish writer (Ngāpuhi/Manase) born and raised in Tāmaki Makaurau Auckland. She is a poet, storyteller and amateur astrologer. Her work has been published both in print and online.

Laura Ferguson lives and works in Te Whanganui-a-Tara Wellington, where she writes in her spare time. She has a cat, an imagination, too many board games and is working on her first novel.

Catherine Fitchett lives in Ōtautahi Christchurch. She is currently revising her first full-length collection, which was long-listed for the John O'Connor Prize for Best First Book of Poetry. 'Chlorine' is one of an ongoing series of poems based on elements of the periodic table.

Alexandra Fraser's poetry has been published in various places for many years, and she is currently rescuing an old A-frame house while working on her third poetry collection.

Amber French grew up in Waitakaruru, Hauraki Plains. She now lives in Tāmaki Makaurau Auckland and works at a university library.

John Gallas is a New Zealand poet, published by Carcanet. His many published books include *40 Lies*, *The Little Sublime Comedy*, *Star City*, *52 Euros*, *The Song Atlas* and *17 Paper Resurrections*. John is a Fellow of the English Association, a St Magnus Orkney Festival poet, a librettist and translator, and is presently volunteer poet for the Sutton Hoo Saxonship building and the John Clare 'The Meeting' projects.

Maryana Garcia is a journalist, poet and picture-maker who is fascinated by everyday miracles. Her poetry has been published in *A Clear Dawn: New Asian Voices from Aotearoa New Zealand*, *Ko Aotearoa Tatou*, *takahē* and *Poetry New Zealand Yearbook*, and her photography has been published in *Stasis*.

John Geraets is a Whangārei-based writer whose *Everything's Something in Place* was published by Titus Books in 2019. An earlier version of his essay was published in *Jacket2*.

Michael Giacon is a Tāmaki Makaurau Auckland-based poet from a large Pākehā-Italian family. In 2016 he graduated with a master's in creative writing from Auckland University of Technology Te Wānanga Aronui o Tāmaki Makaurau, and the same year won the Kathleen Grattan Prize for a Sequence of Poems. He has had work published most recently in *Fast Fibres 9* and *remake 4*.

Eliana Gray is a poet who lives in Ōtepoti Dunedin. Their work has been published online and in *Poetry New Zealand Yearbook*, *Landfall* and *Mayhem*.

Ted Greensmith-West is a writer and solicitor based in Tāmaki Makaurau Auckland who specialises in human rights and Te Tiriti ō Waitangi law. His writing seeks to embrace the dark, the camp and the queer experience. He is currently working on his first collection of poems.

Paula Harris lives in Palmerston North, where she writes and sleeps a lot, because that's what depression makes you do. She won the 2018 Janet B. McCabe Poetry Prize and the 2017 Lilian Ida Smith Award. Her writing has been published in various journals locally and internationally, including *The Sun*, *Diode*, *Passages North*, *New Delta Review* and *Aotearotica*.

Rebecca Hawkes is Methven born and Te Whanganui-a-Tara Wellington based. Her first book, *Meat Lovers*, was published by Auckland University Press in 2022, and her chapbook *Softcore coldsores* was published in *AUP New Poets 5*. She co-edits the journal *Sweet Mammalian* with Nikki-Lee Birdsey, is a founding member of popstar poetry performance posse Show Ponies, and was co-editor of *No Other Place to Stand*, an anthology of poetry on climate change (Auckland University Press, 2022).

Liam Hinton is a Kirikiriroa Hamilton-based poet. His work has been published in *Mayhem*, *Poetry New Zealand Yearbook* and *Starling*. He co-runs One Question Theatre.

Chris Holdaway is a poet and bookmaker from Te Tai Tokerau Northland. He is the author of *Gorse Poems* (Titus Books, 2022) and directs the poetry publishing house Compound Press in Tāmaki Makaurau Auckland.

Alice Hooton lives in Mairangi Bay, Tāmaki Makaurau Auckland. She has been published in New Zealand and overseas.

Lily Holloway was raised in Ōtautahi Christchurch. Their first chapbook was published in 2021 as a part of *AUP New Poets 8*, and their other work can be found in places such as *Cordite*, *Peach Mag*, *HAD*, *Starling* and *Ōrongohau | Best New Zealand Poems*. They are in their first year of an MFA in creative writing at Syracuse University.

Mark Houlahan teaches in the English programme at Te Kura Toi School of Arts, University of Waikato Te Whare Wānanga o Waikato. He is very glad there are still new books of poems to hold in the hand and read.

Evie Howell likes positive affirmation and lines that have double meaning. She is currently writing her thesis and book.

Gail Ingram is an award-winning writer from the Port Hills of Ōtautahi Christchurch and is the author of *Contents Under Pressure* (Pūkeko Publications, 2019). Her poetry and short stories have appeared widely across Aotearoa and in Australia, UK and US. She is the managing editor of *a fine line* and an editor for *Flash Frontier: An Adventure in Short Fiction*.

Shaynah Jackson is a PhD candidate in English literature at the University of Waikato Te Whare Wānanga o Waikato. Her research focuses on queer theory, selfhood and nihilism. She is the creator of Hamilton writing group Queer Writers and is published in *Disability Experiences* and *Modernists on Modernism: An Anthology* (Bloomsbury, 2020).

Lincoln Jaques' poetry, fiction and travel writing has appeared in Aotearoa and internationally, most recently in *TOUGH, Noir Nation, Poetry New Zealand Yearbook, Mayhem, Blackmail Press* and *Poetry for the Planet: An Anthology of Imagined Futures* (Litoria Press, 2021). He was a finalist and highly commended in the 2018 New Voices Emerging Poets Competition and was a 2020 Vaughan Park Residential Scholar. He lives in Tāmaki Makaurau Auckland.

Claudia Jardine is a writer and musician who grew up in Ōtautahi Christchurch. Her debut poetry chapbook, *The Temple of Your Girl*, was published in 2020 in *AUP New Poets 7*, and her writing can be found in many Aotearoa literary journals and on poetry websites. Her new book, *BITER*, will be published by Auckland University Press in 2023.

Amanda Joshua has been published in *Starling, Sweet Mammalian, The Friday Poem, Blackmail Press, Kate Magazine, Craccum, Tarot, Turbine | Kapohau, foam:e, London Grip* and *Poetry New Zealand Yearbook*.

Hebe Kearney (they/them) is a poet who lives in Tāmaki Makaurau Auckland. Their work has appeared in several publications including *Mayhem, Starling, Tarot* and *takahē*.

Tessa Keenan (Te Ātiawa) was raised in Taranaki and is studying law and English at Te Herenga Waka Victoria University of Wellington. She has previously been published in *Starling, a fine line* and *Salient*.

Robert Kempen lives in Tāmaki Makaurau Auckland and has been published in several poetry journals.

Erik Kennedy (he/him) is the author of two poetry collections: *Another Beautiful Day Indoors* (2022) and *There's No Place Like the Internet in Springtime* (2018), both with Te Herenga Waka University Press. He co-edited *No Other Place to Stand*, an anthology of climate change poetry from Aotearoa and the Pacific (Auckland University Press, 2022). Originally from New Jersey, he lives in Ōtautahi Christchurch.

Ana Maria King (Ngāti Maniapoto, Waikato) lives in Te Kūiti with her sister, nephew and mother.

Paula King lives by the Tararua and Ruahine ranges painting, teaching, writing and gardening. Her work has been published in *Turbine | Kapohau, Poetry New Zealand Yearbook, Swamp, Flash Frontier, the unexpected greenness of trees* (Caselberg Trust, 2016) and elsewhere. In 2014 she won the *takahē* poetry prize and in 2016 completed a master's in creative writing at the International Institute of Modern Letters.

Brent Kininmont's poetry can be found in various places, including *Poetry New Zealand Yearbook* and *Ōrongohau | Best New Zealand Poems*. His collection *Thuds Underneath* was published in 2015 by Te Herenga Waka University Press.

Elizabeth (Libby) Kirkby-McLeod is an Aotearoa New Zealand author whose poetry and writing has appeared in a range of New Zealand journals, online publications and in a public art installation. She has written several books, including her poetry collection *Family Instructions Upon Release* (The Cuba Press, 2019) and the children's series *Eugene's Island.* She edited *Lit: Stories from home* (OneTree House, 2021).

Elisabeth Kumar is a lecturer in the University of Auckland's medical humanities programme and recently qualified as a kaiwhakaora ngangahau occupational therapist at Auckland University of Technology Te Wānanga Aronui o Tāmaki Makaurau. She is particularly interested in literature on disability, madness and dialogue.

Katrina Larsen is a poet from Tauranga. She has previously been published in *Blackmail Press, a fine line, takahē* and *Poetry New Zealand Yearbook.*

Jessica Le Bas has published two collections of poetry: *Incognito* and *Walking to Africa* (Auckland University Press, 2007 and 2009). She won the Sarah Broom Prize for Poetry in 2019. Her 2010 children's novel *Staying Home: My True Diary of Survival* was re-released by Penguin Random House in 2021 as *Locked Down.* She lives in Nelson.

Wes Lee lives in Te Whanganui-a-Tara Wellington. She has written three poetry collections and has won a number of awards for her writing. Most recently she was awarded the *Poetry New Zealand* Poetry Prize (2019), and was shortlisted for the NZSA Peter and Dianne Beaton Fellowship (2022); the Alastair Reid Pamphlet Prize (2022); the NZSA Laura Solomon Cuba Press Prize (2022); the Booranga Prize for Best Poem (2022); and the Heroines/Joyce Parkes Women's Writing Prize (2022).

Terry Locke is emeritus professor of arts and language education at the University of Auckland Waipapa Taumata Rau. He has published five books of poetry and edited three anthologies. His last two books, both published by Steele Roberts Aotearoa, were *Ranging Around the Zero* (2014) and *Tending the Landscape of the Heart* (2019). He lives in the Ngongotahā Valley.

Rachel Lockwood is from Hawke's Bay and lives in Te Whanganui-a-Tara Wellington. She has been published in *Starling, Stasis, Milly Magazine, Sour Cherry* and *NZ Poetry Shelf.*

Olivia Macassey is a poet and editor whose work has appeared in *A Pandemic Moment in Time, takahē, Poetry New Zealand Yearbook, Landfall, Otoliths* and other places. She has written two books of poetry.

Abigail Marshall is a writer based in Kirikiriroa Hamilton. Her poems and short stories can be found in *Mayhem, Flash Frontier* and *Landfall.*

Finn McWhirter is based in Tāmaki Makaurau Auckland and lives his life by the motto 'be vulnerable or die'. His most recent work has been published in *Overcommunicate, Six Cents* and *Sour Cherry.*

Lucy Miles is a journalist, English teacher and writer who lives in Tāmaki Makaurau Auckland, where she completed a master's in English literature.

Khadro Mohamed is a writer and poet from Te Whanganui-a-Tara Wellington. She has published in various online magazines, and her book *We're All Made of Lightning* (We Are Babies) was released in 2022.

Margaret Moores lives in Tāmaki Makaurau Auckland, where she and her husband own an indie bookshop. Her poems and flash fiction have been published in journals and anthologies in Aotearoa New Zealand and Australia.

Josiah Morgan is an arts facilitator for The White Room Creative Space, supporting artists with intellectual disabilities to better integrate into the community. He is also a performance artist, critic, producer, writer and actor. His third and fourth books, *The Texas Chainsaw Massacre* (Amphetamine Sulphate) and *Road: A Postlapsarian Comedy* (Feral Dove Press) were both released in 2022.

Elizabeth Morton is a teller of poems and tall tales. She has three collections of poetry — most recently *Naming the Beasts* (Otago University Press, 2022). She has an MLitt in creative writing from the University of Glasgow, and is completing a master's in applied neuroscience.

Emma Neale lives in Ōtepoti Dunedin, where she works as a freelance editor. In 2020 she received the Lauris Edmond Memorial Award in recognition of her distinguished contribution to poetry in Aotearoa New Zealand. *The Pink Jumpsuit: Short Fictions, Tall Truths* (Quentin Wilson Publishing, 2021), her first collection of short fiction, was long-listed for the Jann Medlicott Acorn Prize for Fiction at the 2021 Ockham New Zealand Book Awards.

Ellis Ophele is a US and Aotearoa New Zealand citizen who writes about being transgender, disabled and mentally ill. His work has been published in *Starling* and *Poetry New Zealand Yearbook.*

Claire Orchard lives in Te Whanganui-a-Tara Wellington. Her poetry collection *Cold Water Cure* was published by Te Herenga Waka University Press in 2016. More of her work can be found in *Ōrongohau | Best New Zealand Poems, Landfall, Mayhem, Sweet Mammalian* and *Turbine | Kapohau.*

A. L. Ping's family came to Aotearoa from China in the 1950s. He started writing poetry at the age of six; his work has been published in journals and he has had success in poetry competitions in Australia.

Michele Powles is a writer, dancer, producer and mother. Her fiction, nonfiction and poetry have been published widely and short works have been broadcast for radio in Aotearoa New Zealand and the UK. She was the 2010 Robert Burns Fellow and has a number of screen works in development.

Mark Prisco's poems have been published in journals since 2016. He was guest editor for *Mayhem* in 2021 and his reviews have been published in *Poetry New Zealand Yearbook.*

Grace Prodanov is 21 years old. You can find her previous work on the internet.

Hayden Pyke was born and raised in Waikato and lives with his family on the ancestral whenua of Te Kawerau ā Maki in Waitākere, Tāmaki Makaurau Auckland. His short fiction and poetry has been published in journals such as *Landfall* and *Mayhem.*

Erin Ramsay is a poet ambiguously located, who is completing a master's in history at Te Herenga Waka Victoria University of Wellington.

essa may ranapiri (Ngaati Raukawa, Te Arawa, Ngaati Pukeko, Clan Gunn) lives on Ngaati Wairere whenua. They are the author of *ransack* and *Echidna*, and the co-editor of *Kupu Toi Takataapui | Takataapui Literary Journal* with Michelle Rahurahu; they will write until they're dead.

Vaughan Rapatahana (Te Ātiawa) spends his time writing and travelling between Aotearoa, Hong Kong SAR, and the Philippines.

Robyn Restieaux is a writer based in Tāmaki Makaurau Auckland. She has taught English literature for years and is now immersed in her own craft. Her work was most recently published in the Aotearoa poetry journal *Tarot.*

Clare Riddell is a poet based in Kemureti Cambridge. She has recently completed her bachelor of arts with honours in English at the University of Waikato Te Whare Wānanga o Waikato.

Heidi Rogers grew up telling stories to her 'invisible audience'. She is a PhD candidate at the University of Waikato Te Whare Wānanga o Waikato and is writing a cli-fi about saving Tāne Mahuta from kauri dieback.

Dadon Rowell is a Kirikiriroa Hamilton-based poet and short fiction writer. Her work has featured in multiple journals and anthologies including *Mayhem, Poetry New Zealand Yearbook, Sweet Mammalian, Starling* and *No Other Place to Stand* (Auckland University Press, 2022). She was recently shortlisted in *Flash Frontier*'s Micro Madness competition.

Harriet Salmon is a poet and student at Te Herenga Waka Victoria University of Wellington. She has previously been published in *Starling, takahē* and *a fine line.*

Lisa Samuels works with experimental writing, interactive art and relational theory in transnational life. Her recent books are *The Long White Cloud of Unknowing* (Chax Press, 2019) and *Breach* (Boiler House Press, 2021), and a Serbian translation of her novel *Tender Girl* was published as *Mekana Devojka* (Partizanska, 2022). A new poetry collection, *Livestream*, is forthcoming in 2023.

Kerrin P. Sharpe has had four collections of poetry published with Te Herenga Waka University Press. Her work has also appeared in *Ōrongohau | Best New Zealand Poems, Oxford Poets 13, Blackbox Manifold, POETRY* (US) and in *PN Review*. In 2020 she was shortlisted for the Alpine Fellowship Writing Prize and she was awarded a Michael King Writers Centre Summer Residency in 2021.

Charlotte Simmonds is an autistic writer, translator and science editor in Te Whanganui-a-Tara Wellington. Their work has been widely published in Australia, the US and Aotearoa. *The World's Fastest Flower*, a collection of poetry and lyric prose, was published by Te Herenga Waka University Press in 2008.

Jane Simpson is an Ōtautahi Christchurch-based poet and historian who has published two collections: *A world without maps* and *Tuning Wordsworth's Piano* (Interactive Publications, 2016 and 2019), and a self-published liturgy, *The Farewelling of a Home* (2021). Her poems have most recently appeared in *Allegro, London Grip, Hamilton Stone Review, Otoliths, Poetry New Zealand Yearbook* and *Catalyst.*

Nigel Skjellerup works in the Ōtautahi Christchurch healthcare community. He has been published in *The Press, takahē, New Zealand Poetry Society Anthology, Anesthesia and Analgesia*'s 'The Human Experience', *Mayhem* and *Poetry New Zealand Yearbook.*

Kim Slemint recently returned to Aotearoa New Zealand after 29 years abroad. She has previously been published in *Poetry New Zealand Yearbook, Trout, JAAM, Mountain Gazette* and various other US publications.

Elizabeth Smither's latest collection *My American Chair* was published in Aotearoa in 2022 by Auckland University Press and in the US by MadHat Press.

Michael Steven is the author of numerous poetry collections and chapbooks. His most recent book *Night School* won the 2021 Kathleen Grattan Award for Poetry.

Shaun Stockley lives in Manawatū. His interest in poetry began as a child in England, and he was published twice in *Young Writers* (2004 and 2006). Now home in Aotearoa New Zealand, he uses poetry to explore and challenge his relationship with the country.

Melinda Szymanik is a Tāmaki Makaurau Auckland-based award-winning writer of poetry and children's fiction, including short stories, picture books and novels. Her poetry has also appeared in *Poetry New Zealand Yearbook, takahē* and *NZ Poetry Shelf.*

Loren Thomas is a writer originally from Te Tai Tokerau. She has been published in *Poetry New Zealand Yearbook, Mayhem, Starling* and *The Spinoff*'s 'The Friday Poem'.

Isaiah Tiuka (Ngāi Tūhoe, Ngāti Kahungunu) was born in Hawke's Bay and now lives in Te Whanganui-a-Tara Wellington. They recently finished a bachelor's degree in psychology and criminology and are pursuing a master's in health.

Catherine Trundle is a writer from Te Whanganui-a-Tara Wellington. Her poetry and flash fiction have appeared in a number of Australasian publications, including *Landfall, Not Very Quiet, Flash Frontier, takahē* and *Poetry New Zealand Yearbook.*

Feana Tu'akoi is the 2022 Massey University Writer in Residence and the recipient of the 2022 Storylines Tom Fitzgibbon Award for her original mid-grade novel manuscript *A Perfect Failure.*

Rhegan Tu'akoi is a Tongan and Pākehā writer who lives in Te Whanganui-a-Tara Wellington. Her family hails from the grassy plains of South Canterbury, and the beautiful village of Holonga, Tongatapu. She has recently been published in *The Pantograph Punch, Sweet Mammalian* and *Mayhem.*

Richard von Sturmer is an Aotearoa New Zealand writer. His recent collection of poetry and prose *Resonating Distances* (Titus Books) was published in 2022. In 2020 he was the University of Waikato Te Whare Wānanga o Waikato writer in residence.

Janet Wainscott lives near Ōtautahi Christchurch and writes poetry and essays. Her poetry has appeared in publications including *takahē, Landfall, Catalyst, Shot Glass Journal* and in recent New Zealand Poetry Society anthologies and *Poetry New Zealand Yearbook.*

Hannah Wilson is a graduate of Raphael House Rudolf Steiner School. Their poem 'Medusa' won first prize in the 2022 *Poetry New Zealand Yearbook* Student Poetry Competition.

Laura Williamson is a writer, performer and poet based in Central Otago. She edits the magazine *1964* and co-wrote 'The Blue Moments Project', a song and spoken word cycle. Her book *The Bike and Beyond: Life on Two Wheels in Aotearoa New Zealand* was published by Bridget Williams Books in 2016.

Sophia Wilson is based near Ōtepoti Dunedin, where she runs a rural property and animal refuge with her partner and daughters. She was awarded the inaugural Flying Islands Manuscript Prize *En Cas D'Urgence* in 2022. Her collection *Sea Skins* is forthcoming in 2023.

Tim Wilson has lived in Pōkeno, Fitzroy, Whanganui, Tokyo, Seoul, Brooklyn and Manhattan. He now lives with his wife, Rachel, and their four boys in Tāmaki Makaurau Auckland.

Sue Wootton lives in Ōtepoti Dunedin. Her most recent publications are a novel, *Strip* (Mākaro Press, 2016), and a poetry collection, *The Yield* (Otago University Press, 2017), which were longlisted and shortlisted respectively at the Ockham New Zealand Book Awards.

David Wrigley is a writer and musician whose poetry, short stories and criticism have appeared in various literary and food journals in Aotearoa and the UK. He is working on a novel. He lives with his partner and two sons in Kemureti Cambridge.

Chantelle Xiong is a year 12 student at St Andrew's College, Ōtautahi Christchurch. Their poem 'Aged' won first prize in the 2022 *Poetry New Zealand Yearbook* Student Poetry Competition.

Poetry New Zealand Yearbook, founded by Louis Johnson in 1951, is New Zealand's longest-running poetry magazine. It has been edited by some of New Zealand's most distinguished poets and academics, including Elizabeth Caffin, Grant Duncan, Riemke Ensing, Bernard Gadd, Leonard Lambert, Harry Ricketts, Elizabeth Smither, Brian Turner, Alistair Paterson, Jack Ross and Johanna Emeney. It is now edited by Dr Tracey Slaughter of Te Whare Wānanga o Waikato University of Waikato. The university's financial support of the yearbook is much appreciated. In 2023 the yearbook was renamed *Poetry Aotearoa Yearbook.*

Managing editor: Tracey Slaughter
editor@poetrynz.net; website: www.poetrynz.net

Submissions: The submission dates for each issue are between 1 May and 31 July of each year. Email submissions are preferred and should go, with a covering letter, to editor@poetrynz.net. Please paste your poems in the body of the message or include them as a single MS Word file attachment.

Submissions by post and a covering letter should be sent to: Dr Tracey Slaughter, English Programme, School of Arts, University of Waikato, Private Bag 3105, Hamilton 3240. Posted submissions will not be returned.

Please include a short biography and your current postal address with your submission. Contributors whose poems are selected will receive a free copy of the issue in which their work is included.

First published in 2023 by Massey University Press
Private Bag 102904, North Shore Mail Centre
Auckland 0745, New Zealand
www.masseypress.ac.nz

Cover design by Jo Bailey, Thomas Cumming and Krista Barnaby
Typesetting by Megan van Staden

Extracts published with permission:
Page 138: 'Do not go gentle into that good night', by Dylan Thomas, courtesy of Dylan Thomas' estate; page 206: 'What I'd like', by J. C. Sturm, courtesy of J. C. Sturm's estate; page 222: 'Canto LXXXI', by Ezra Pound, courtesy of Faber & Faber; page 253–54, 'A Short Film', by Ted Hughes, courtesy of Faber & Faber.

A catalogue record for this book is available from the National Library of New Zealand

Printed and bound in China by Everbest Printing Investment Limited

ISBN: 978-1-99-101635-5

The assistance of Creative New Zealand is gratefully acknowledged by the publisher

Poetry Aotearoa Yearbook 2023 is published in association with Te Whare Wānanga o Waikato University of Waikato